PENGUIN BOOKS

michelle bridges'
australian
calorie counter

T0363636

michelle bridges'

australian

calorie counter

Penguin Books

PENGUIN BOOKS

UK | USA | Canada | Ireland | Australia
India | New Zealand | South Africa | China

Penguin Books is part of the Penguin Random House group of companies
whose addresses can be found at global.penguinrandomhouse.com.

First published by Penguin Books Australia Ltd, 1992
This edition published by Penguin Group (Australia), 2013

Cover design by Adam Laszczuk © Penguin Group (Australia)
Cover photograph by Nick Wilson
Printed and bound in Australia by Griffin Press, an accredited ISO AS/NZS
14001 Environmental Management Systems printer.

A catalogue record for this
book is available from the
National Library of Australia

ISBN 978 0 14356 824 7

penguin.com.au

contents

Introduction

Your approach to food is the key ingredient in moving you closer to your weight, fitness and health goals. Understanding the nutritional and energy values of the foods you eat is *crucial* to managing your weight. The basic premise is simple – take in more calories than you burn off, and the excess is stored as fat. And when you do this over a long period of time, bingo! We're talking overweight or obese, as well as a higher likelihood of illness and disease. The bottom line is that KNOWLEDGE IS POWER! When you learn which foods are high in nutrients and low in calories, you can start to make smarter choices and become a healthier, slimmer you.

What should you eat?

It's no coincidence that healthy foods that are *high* in nutrients are usually *low* in calories. This means you can eat a lot of them with a clear conscience, helping you stay in control of your weight *and* feel amazing in the process. You'll have more energy and your body will be getting all the vitamins, minerals and nutrients it needs to function at its optimum level. Healthy foods are often referred to as 'wholefoods' because they've undergone minimal (if any) processing and contain no preservatives or added salts, sugars, etc. They've literally been pulled straight from the ground, fished from the sea, or plucked from a tree.

Fruit, vegetables, fish, lean meats and wholegrain cereals, breads and crackers are the staples of a wholefood diet (add nuts and legumes if you're a vegetarian). Here's an example of a wholefood-rich menu plan that will keep you feeling full, but ensures that your calories stay down. Notice that only around 30 per cent of the calorie/kilojoule intake occurs in the afternoon and evening, with the majority taken in during the first seven or eight hours of the day. This fits with the principle of 'eat like a king for breakfast, like a prince for lunch and like a pauper for dinner'.

A Sample Menu Plan

	KJ	CAL
Breakfast		
1 chopped pear	252	60
1 chopped kiwi fruit	168	40
100 g blueberries	210	50
1 tub of low-calorie yoghurt	336	80
1 coffee with high-calcium skim milk	420	100
Morning snack		
2 carrots	168	40
2 sticks celery	42	10
4 tablespoons low-calorie cottage cheese	504	120
2 small rice crackers	126	30

Lunch

Large bowl mixed leafy green salad (approx. 3 cups)	210	50
1 tomato	84	20
2 raw mushrooms	42	10
10 grapes	84	20
10 slices cucumber	42	10
180 g tuna in spring water	840	200
1 tablespoon olive oil (optional)	420	100

Afternoon snack

1 sliced pear	252	60
4 Vita-Weat crackers	378	90
1 tea with high-calcium skim milk	126	30

Dinner

Chicken stir-fry:		
150 g lean chicken breast	840	200
3 cups steamed mixed vegetables (green/red/yellow)	420	100
1 orange	336	80

Total energy intake = 6300 kilojoules (1500 calories)

How much should you eat?

The answer to this is simple – A LOT LESS! Unfortunately, the increase in our consumption of calorie-dense food has been coupled with a significant increase in our portion sizes. We simply eat too much, but most of us have been eating this way for so long that we don't even realise it. It's another reason to pay careful attention to the calories in your meals.

The number of calories you need to maintain good health depends on how active you are, your height and weight, your age and your gender. Clearly, more calories are needed when the body is growing during adolescence, or if you're running around after kids and working full-time as well, but what many people don't realise is that your calorie intake should decrease as you age. The table below shows recommended daily intake.

age	FEMALES		MALES	
	calories	kilojoules	calories	kilojoules
14–18	1800–2300	7560–9660	2300–3300	9660–13860
19–30	1300–1800	5460–7560	1800–2800	7560–11760
31–50	1300–1600	5460–6720	1600–2500	6720–10500
51–70	1300–1500	5460–6300	1500–2500	6300–10500
70+	1300–1500	5460–6300	1500–2000	6300–8400

Source: National Health & Medical Research Council

Tips for managing your weight

One way or another, everything you put into your body will either be converted into energy to fuel body functions and movement or converted to your butt size. That's why people who make poor food choices stay overweight even though they're training hard. While exercise will do amazing things for your mind, your body and your spirit, *losing weight will always come down to what you put in your mouth*! End of story! If I had two clients, one of whom refused to eat well and ate whatever she liked, but trained like a demon every day, and another who did *no* exercise but tidied up her diet, the non-exerciser would lose the most weight. Of course the best scenario is the double-whammy approach: good nutrition *plus* exercise.

1. Get real

I've said it before and I'll say it again: healthy food and regular exercise are the keys to managing your weight, and therefore your health and wellbeing. We know this, so why are nine million Australians overweight? In my experience, one reason we struggle with our weight is that we haven't addressed the emotional issues behind our poor eating habits. It's time to come clean about the behaviours that have been holding you back from healthy eating and healthy living. All the excuses about why you can't eat healthily or exercise – they have to GO!

The sooner they're out of your life, the sooner you can move forward, so instead of living in denial and pretending everything's fine, try facing up to some truths. If your blood pressure or your cholesterol is high, or you've gone up two clothing sizes, or you can't walk up a flight of stairs without heaving up a lung, it's time to make some changes!

2. Set your goal

First, you need to get on the scales, get out the tape measure, and go to your doctor for a full check-up. Gather all the results and keep them in a journal.

Now, work out exactly what your goal is, but bear in mind that you're not going to stop your new healthy way of life once you achieve that goal, okay? The commitment is to changing your lifestyle in the long-term, but short-term goals are brilliant for motivating you. Work out your healthy weight range (see the body mass index charts in my book *Crunch Time* or at my website michellebridges.com.au), and set a fitness target. Next, mark on your calendar a realistic date for you to reach your goal and write down what you need to achieve each week to get there. I repeat, be *realistic* – but determined! You'll feel amazing when you start to see the numbers going down. It's about as motivating as you can get!

3. Keep a food diary

Write down everything you eat and drink for seven days. Don't diet – just eat what you'd normally eat, but write it all down with absolute honesty. This is where you'll learn about what's got you to where you are today. Then use the *Michelle Bridges' Australian Calorie Counter* to add up all the calories you've ingested over the week. It's a great eye-opener!

When you start a new, healthier eating program, continue with the food diary and record your calories. You'll see how much better you are doing and realise that you don't need so many calories to feel full or energised.

4. Clean up your diet

For many of us, it's time to grow up and stop eating like a teenager whose parents have gone away for the weekend! Allow yourself one 'treat' meal a week so you don't feel like you're missing out, but for the rest of your meals, eat lots of fresh fruit and vegetables, fish and lean meat (or pulses and nuts if you're a vegetarian), plus lightly processed cereals.

Also, you MUST eat breakfast, lunch *and* dinner. Skipping meals only gives you the opportunity to play your old games. You know the ones: 'Well, I've hardly eaten all day, so now I can gorge myself' or 'Well, if I skip breakfast and only have an apple for lunch, then I can tuck into a smorgasbord and a crate of beer'. So give up the games. If you eat three good meals a day, you'll find you only have a snack during the day if you need the energy, and you'll no longer binge at night. Focus on eating more during the day when you need it, and less at night.

5. Control your portions

Take a hard look at your portions – there's a good chance you're eating much more than you need. You may have been eating hefty meals for so long that you don't even realise how big they are! Yes, cutting them down is going to be a little uncomfortable at first. You've trained your stomach to expect *way* more than it needs, so it's probably going to let you know how it feels about the new portions. But you won't die! You'll still be able to fill your belly, but it will be with nutrient-dense, low-calorie wholefoods. To help with portion control, follow these simple rules: use smaller plates; *never* go back for seconds; *never* eat while you're cooking; and *never* eat the leftovers – save them for lunch the next day (which will also save you money!).

6. Get cooking

There's no way you can accelerate yourself to lean and mean unless you put in some time in the kitchen. Not only is cooking easy, it also means you take responsibility for your own nutrition, and that's an important step towards taking responsibility for your body. And if you have children, teaching them to cook will give them essential skills for a healthier, happier life.

Learning to put a few simple meals together will not only save you stacks of money, but is a critical part of taking control of your diet. If you're not used to cooking, my books *Crunch Time*, *Crunch Time Cookbook*, *Losing the Last 5 Kilos* and *The No Excuses Cookbook* have some really simple, delicious recipes. Trust me: the more you cook, the easier it gets.

7. Get moving

Exercise is the fountain of youth. Research shows that it not only acts as a preventative, relieving you of stresses and anxieties that can bring about illness, but also has curative properties. Exercise makes you stronger, fitter and lighter, so you get to live a more productive and active life for *longer*.

It's actually unnatural for us *not* to exercise, and we're seeing the results of inactivity in surging levels of obesity, mental illness, diabetes, heart disease and the other illnesses that have evolved and multiplied as a result of our sedentary lifestyles.

Clearly, exercise does a lot more than help you lose weight. Still, if weight-loss is your number-one goal, then exercise is the way to go! But it's got to be intense – the harder you're puffing, the better, because the harder your heart's pumping, the more calories you're burning. And it's important to keep challenging your body; that way you will continue to see improvement and avoid plateaus. You can find workout programs and ideas in my books *Crunch Time* and *Losing the Last 5 Kilos.*

8. Break bad habits

We make and break habits all the time. If you've been able to develop poor eating or exercise habits, then you're equally able to develop healthy ones. You need to 'outmanoeuvre' your weaknesses. Perhaps it means:

- Turning off the TV two nights a week and going for a walk or a bike ride instead.
- Popping a couple of apples in your handbag, so you're not tempted to go to a chip and soft-drink machine.
- Brushing your teeth straight after dinner – it puts a full stop on the meal so you won't go back for seconds.
- Rewarding yourself with anything other than food. And that goes for your kids, too.

Frequently asked questions
Should I follow a low-carbohydrate diet?

In a word – no. Carbohydrates give us energy and keep our brains functioning optimally – when there aren't enough of them in our diet, we can get tired and cranky. Most of us think of carbs as being in foods like bread, pasta, biscuits and cereals. We forget that fruit and vegetables also have carbs – that's why we feel full when we eat a decent serve of them. Make better carbohydrate choices with low-GI (low glycaemic index) foods, wholemeal breads and brown rice. Eat most of your carbs in the morning and at lunchtime when you need the energy.

Should I follow a low-GI diet?

The glucose in low-GI carbs is absorbed slowly by our bodies, meaning we produce less insulin. One of the functions of insulin is to instruct our bodies to store fat, so diabetics and people trying to lose weight should choose low-GI carbs wherever possible. Low-GI foods include mixed-grain breads, oats, legumes, milk, yoghurt and most fruit. High-GI foods include white bread, potatoes, white rice, biscuits and cakes.

Should I count the fat in food rather than the calories?

Since fat is calorie-dense, low-calorie food is usually low in fat anyway. If you want to lose weight, your primary interest should be the total calorie content of the food you're eating. Remember that much of the food labelled 'low fat' is still high in carbohydrates or sugar, and therefore still high in calories.

What's the best form of exercise for losing weight?

Anything that ups your heart rate and gets you sweating. You should do a mix of weight training and cardio. Weight training increases your fat-burning furnace – your muscles! The more lean muscle you have, the more calories you'll burn. Combine weight training with fitness training like running and skipping.

How often should I exercise?

Our bodies are designed to be active so move them as much as possible. I get all my clients to commit to six training sessions a week. Three will be hard sessions, two medium-intensity and one will be light, such as a walk or a yoga class. Incidental exercise will also help you reach your goal – you can burn a truckload of calories doing the housework, taking the stairs instead of the lift, or taking the dog for a walk. Choose to move!

How do I stay motivated?

Nothing motivates like success! Don't let those sneaky excuses come back into your life. It's easy to fall into the trap of thinking about exercise so much that you talk yourself out of it! While it's great to have goals, accept that there will be days when you are uninspired. When I feel that way, I get into 'robot mode'. I just put my shoes on and go. If I start to think about it, I can come up with loads of excuses as to why I should put it off.

How to use this book

There are thousands of products listed in the *Michelle Bridges' Australian Calorie Counter*, so to make it easier to find your way around, I've arranged them in broad categories (e.g. drinks, vegetables, breakfast cereals, bread, etc.). Within each category, individual food types and brands are listed alphabetically. As your first choice should always be fresh wholefoods, these have been listed first wherever possible.

Quantities given reflect either typical package sizes or, where package sizes or serving sizes vary, a consistent measure. Sometimes common quantities or measurements are used. Remember, these are not recommended portion sizes, just the best way to measure the calorie count.

I have tried to include as many popular food products as possible, but don't let any omissions prevent you from finding out the calorie/kilojoule count of everything you eat and drink. Ultimately, you are responsible for what you put in your mouth.

Good luck!

Drinks

Be careful of alcoholic drinks – they're loaded with calories and have almost no nutritional value. It's also easy to make poor food choices if you've had a few too many. Soft drinks and cordials should be a very occasional treat, as reaching for them whenever you're thirsty will substantially increase your daily calorie count. Try to avoid making them the default drink at dinner, so the kids don't expect it every day. Always check the kilojoule/calorie content of drinks, even juices, and beware those that contain sucrose or corn syrup – these are refined sugars that your body finds hard to break down, and they're the worst offenders in terms of calorie load. When it comes to diet drinks, there is research out there about the negative effects of artificial sweeteners on the body, so keep them to a minimum if you feel you can't live without them. Also, watch out for coffees from takeaway chains that have had creams and syrups added. To be honest, you just can't beat water!

	PORTION SIZE	KJ	CAL

alcoholic drinks

ale

CARLTON...black	375 ml	585	140
JAMES SQUIRE			
golden ale	375 ml	615	146
amber ale	375 ml	701	191

beer

ASAHI	330 ml	558	132
CARLTON COLD...lager	375 ml	581	138
CASCADE...premium	330 ml	554	132
CASTLEMAINE XXXX			
bitter lager	375 ml	570	136
draught	375 ml	551	135
CORONA...lager	330 ml	584	139
EMU...bitter	375 ml	626	150
EUMUNDI...lager	375 ml	618	146
FOSTERS...lager	375 ml	630	150
HAHN...premium lager	330 ml	568	135
HEINEKEN...lager	330 ml	561	132
MELBOURNE...bitter	375 ml	592	142
SOUTHWARK...premium	375 ml	630	150
STELLA ARTOIS...lager	330 ml	601	142
SWAN...draught	375 ml	573	138
TOOHEYS...new	375 ml	603	142
VICTORIA BITTER...lager	375 ml	630	150

	PORTION SIZE	KJ	CAL
beer, reduced-alcohol			
CASCADE...premium light	375 ml	446	105
CASTLEMAINE XXXX			
gold	375 ml	453	108
light bitter	375 ml	371	93
FOSTERS...lite ice	375 ml	435	103
HAHN...premium light	375 ml	446	105
WEST END...light	375 ml	390	93
beer, low-carb			
HAHN...super dry	330 ml	416	99
PURE BLONDE...premium lager	355 ml	444	106
TOOHEYS...new...white stag	345 ml	435	103
champagne			
av. all varieties	150 ml	518	124
cider			
MERCURY...dry	345 ml	199	47
STRONGBOW			
dry	100 ml	179	43
sweet	100 ml	244	58
original	100 ml	213	51
cocktails & mixes			
bloody mary; gin & tonic	250 ml	810	195
bourbon & soda	250 ml	950	225
daiquiri; pina colada	250 ml	1945	465
manhattan	250 ml	2350	560
martini	250 ml	1390	335

	PORTION SIZE	**KJ**	**CAL**
screwdriver	250 ml	865	205
tequila sunrise	250 ml	1150	275
tom collins	250 ml	575	135
whisky sour	250 ml	1425	340
liqueurs			
advocaat; cointreau; grand marnier	30 ml	353	84
apricot/peach brandy; kirsch	30 ml	203	49
baileys; creme de menthe; drambuie; kahlua;			
malibu; tia maria	30 ml	375	90
benedictine; chartreuse; galliano; sambuca	30 ml	503	120
cherry brandy	30 ml	323	77
curacao	30 ml	390	93
spirits			
brandy	30 ml	200	48
gin	30 ml	290	69
ouzo	30 ml	345	82
rum	30 ml	420	100
vodka	30 ml	295	71
whisky	30 ml	245	59
stout			
CARBINE	375 ml	708	168
GUINNESS	375 ml	843	201
SOUTHWARK	375 ml	896	217
wines			
chablis; dry white; rosé	150 ml	443	106
champagne	150 ml	525	125

	PORTION SIZE	KJ	CAL
red	150 ml	502	120
riesling; semillon; chardonnay	150 ml	533	127
sauternes	150 ml	563	135
sweet			
red	150 ml	758	181
white	150 ml	630	151
wines, fortified			
port	55 ml	361	86
sherry			
dry	55 ml	256	61
sweet	55 ml	336	80
vermouth			
dry	55 ml	303	72
sweet	55 ml	339	81
wines, low-calorie			
LINDEMANS...early harvest			
crisp dry white	150 ml	308	74
semillon sauvignon blanc	150 ml	321	77
YELLOWGLEN			
bella	150 ml	444	106
jewel yellow	150 ml	249	60

soft drinks

carbonated drinks

AUSTRALIA'S CHOICE			
lemonade	100 ml	199	47

	PORTION SIZE	KJ	CAL
BISLERI			
chinotto	100 ml	189	45
CASCADE			
Appletiser	100 ml	208	50
Grapetiser	100 ml	257	61
premium ginger beer	100 ml	184	44
COCA-COLA			
Coke			
diet	100 ml	1.5	0.3
regular	100 ml	180	43
zero	100 ml	1.4	0.3
DEEP SPRING			
mineral water			
berry waterfall	100 ml	107	25
lemon	100 ml	156	37
orange passionfruit	100 ml	138	33
DIET WATERFORDS			
natural mineral water			
apple berry; green tea; lemon, lime & orange;			
melon & mango; pink grapefruit	100 ml	10	2
FANTA			
orange	100 ml	212	51
zero	100 ml	0	0
KIRKS			
creaming soda	100 ml	176	42
ginger beer	100 ml	214	51

	PORTION SIZE	KJ	CAL
lemon squash	100 ml	193	46
sarsparilla	100 ml	209	50
LIFT			
diet	100 ml	27	7
standard	100 ml	196	47
PEPSI			
Cola	100 ml	197	47
7UP	100 ml	182	43
light	100 ml	1.7	0.5
SAXBYS			
diet ginger beer	100 ml	2	0.5
ginger beer	100 ml	223	53
SCHWEPPES			
agrum...sugar free	100 ml	5	1
bitter lemon	100 ml	226	54
dry ginger ale	100 ml	125	30
Indian tonic water	100 ml	159	38
Indian tonic water...diet	100 ml	6	1.5
lemonade...sugar free	100 ml	5	1
lime & soda	100 ml	82	19
natural mineral water			
apple & pink grapefruit	100 ml	139	33
lemon & lime; orange & passionfruit	100 ml	131	31
traditional			
brown cream soda	250 ml	515	123
ginger beer	250 ml	508	121

	PORTION SIZE	KJ	CAL
lemonade with lemon juice	250 ml	456	109
lime flavour	250 ml	515	123
raspberry flavour	250 ml	538	128
sarsparilla	250 ml	488	117
SOLO			
lemon	100 ml	214	51
sub	100 ml	11	3
lemon lime	100 ml	197	47
sunkist	100 ml	232	56
TARAX			
lemonade	100 ml	143	34

sports & energy drinks

	PORTION SIZE	KJ	CAL
GATORADE			
all flavours	100 ml	105	25
LUCOZADE			
orange	100 ml	298	71
original	100 ml	304	73
POWERADE			
isotonic			
berry ice; lemon lime	100 ml	131	31
mountain blast	100 ml	133	32
sports waters...all flavours	100 ml	44	11
RED BULL	100 ml	192	46
SUSTAGEN SPORT ... 60 g + 200 ml water	260 ml	942	220

	PORTION SIZE	KJ	CAL
coffee			
NB: sugar, 1 level tsp	4 g	65	15
black, espresso, filter, instant	250 ml	25	6
black + 1 sugar	250 ml	45	26
black + 1 sugar + cream (vienna)	250 ml	445	106
caffe latte			
reduced fat	250 ml	420	100
skim milk	250 ml	340	80
whole milk	250 ml	550	130
cappuccino			
reduced fat	250 ml	300	71
skim milk	250 ml	220	52
whole milk	250 ml	380	90
iced coffee			
cream + ice-cream	250 ml	1045	250
whole milk	250 ml	645	154
coffee mixes			
JARRAH			
cappuccino; mocha	15 g	238	56
all other flavours	12 g	238	56
coffee substitute			
CARO	4 g	62	15
tea			
black	250 ml	17	4

	PORTION SIZE	KJ	CAL
black + 1 sugar	250 ml	85	20
white			
with reduced-fat milk	250 ml	70	17
with whole milk	250 ml	90	22
white + 1 sugar			
with reduced-fat milk	250 ml	150	36
with whole milk	250 ml	170	41

tea drinks

LIPTON			
peach	100 ml	592	142
green tea apple	100 ml	120	29
NESTEA…ice tea…peach mango	100 ml	102	24
TETLEY…ice-t			
green tea	100 ml	151	36
lemon & lime	100 ml	99	24
peach & orange	100 ml	150	36
raspberry & cranberry	100 ml	150	36

cordial (diluted)

BICKFORD'S			
bitter lemon	250 ml	399	95
diet lemon	250 ml	21	5
diet lime	250 ml	26	6
lime	250 ml	309	74
peach tea	250 ml	298	71

	PORTION SIZE	KJ	CAL
BOTTLEGREEN			
elderflower; ginger & lemongrass	250 ml	290	67
BUDERIM			
ginger refresher	250 ml	547	137
lime refresher	250 ml	544	130
CASCADE ... ultra C	200 ml	320	76
COTTEE'S ... fruit juice cordial			
apple & blackcurrant crush	250 ml	365	87
blueberry; lime; raspberry	250 ml	291	69
lemon barley crush	250 ml	330	79
low-joule apple & raspberry	250 ml	33	7
GOLDEN CIRCLE			
light...av. all flavours	100 ml	15	4
standard...av. all flavours	100 ml	151	36
RIBENA			
light	100 ml	36	9
regular	100 ml	210	50
SCHWEPPES			
diet lime	100 ml	4	1
lemon juice	100 ml	126	30
WEIGHT WATCHERS ... berry	250 ml	30	7

fruit drinks

BERRI			
cranberry	100 ml	205	49

	PORTION SIZE	KJ	CAL
GOLDEN CIRCLE			
30% fruit nectar			
guava	100 ml	217	52
mango	100 ml	215	51
golden pash	100 ml	199	47
pine coconut; pine orange	100 ml	206	00
pine mango	100 ml	191	46
sunshine punch	100 ml	213	51
tropical punch	100 ml	198	49
SPRING VALLEY			
juice spa			
apple blackcurrant	300 ml	453	108
orange & passionfruit; orange & pineapple	300 ml	435	104
SUNRAYSIA			
cranberry	250 ml	820	195
cranberry diet lite	250 ml	118	28
raspberry	250 ml	585	140
SO JUICY			
orange	100 ml	207	49
orange mango	100 ml	207	49
orange passionfruit	100 ml	207	49

fruit juices

	PORTION SIZE	KJ	CAL
BERRI			
apple mango	100 ml	215	523
orange	100 ml	160	386

	PORTION SIZE	KJ	CAL
no added sugar			
apple; apple & pear	100 ml	180	43
multi-V	100 ml	185	44
orange	100 ml	180	41
pineapple	100 ml	185	44
BICKFORDS			
cranberry	100 ml	224	53
pomegranate	100 ml	269	64
prune	100 ml	244	58
DAILY JUICE			
apple	100 ml	180	43
breakfast juice	100 ml	165	51
FREEDOM FOODS			
organic grape	150 ml	640	152
GOLDEN CIRCLE			
100% juice…av. all flavours	100 ml	250	60
tomato	100 ml	84	20
JUST JUICE			
apple; paradise punch	100 ml	180	43
orange	100 ml	160	38
NUDIE			
orange, carrot & ginger juicie	250 ml	330	79
mango & passionfruit crushie	250 ml	548	130
strawberry & banana crushie	250 ml	593	141
OCEAN SPRAY			
cranberry classic	250 ml	518	124

	PORTION SIZE	KJ	CAL
light cranberry	250 ml	83	20
ruby red grapefruit	250 ml	524	125
ORIGINAL JUICE CO.			
black label			
apple & forest fruits	100 ml	199	48
apple guava	100 ml	215	52
grapefruit	100 ml	177	43
orange	100 ml	178	43
pineapple	100 ml	110	262
PUREHARVEST (organic)			
apple; apple pear	100 ml	172	41
apple strawberry	100 ml	165	39

juice-bar drinks

	PORTION SIZE	KJ	CAL
BOOST			
juices			
av. all varieties			
kids	350 ml	665	158
medium	450 ml	855	204
original	650 ml	1235	294
energiser	100 ml	197	47
two and five	100 ml	139	33
smoothies . . . low fat			
av. all varieties			
kids	350 ml	1008	240
medium	450 ml	1294	308

	PORTION SIZE	KJ	CAL
original	650 ml	1869	445
banana buzz	100 ml	307	73
mango magic	100 ml	285	68
tropical storm	100 ml	274	65

vegetable juices

CAMPBELL'S... V8

apple, carrot & ginger	250 ml	410	98
original (low sodium)	250 ml	188	45
tropical	250 ml	412	99

HARVEY FRESH

carrot juice	250 ml	338	81

vitamin water

GLACEAU

av. all flavours	100 ml	94	22

flavoured milk
See also **Milk, Cheese, Yoghurt**

BIG M

chocolate	250 ml	733	175
strawberry	250 ml	698	167

FARMERS UNION

iced coffee	375 ml	1073	256

MOOVE

chocolate	250 ml	663	158

	PORTION SIZE	KJ	CAL
PAULS			
all natural...av. all flavours	100 ml	305	73
breaka...chocolate	100 ml	370	88
ice break	100 ml	283	67
ice break loaded	100 ml	279	66
iced coffee	100 ml	329	79
rush...av. all flavours	100 ml	196	47
shake	100 ml	403	96
PURA			
IC strong iced coffee	100 ml	299	71
SANITARIUM UP & GO			
vanilla ice; choc ice	350 ml	1190	284

milk-drink mixes

carob powder, 1 tbsp	7 g	23	5
cocoa powder ... av. all brands, 1 tbsp	7 g	90	22
ABUNDANT EARTH			
organic drinking chocolate, 1 tbsp	7 g	106	25
AKTAVITE	15 g	224	53
CADBURY			
drinking chocolate	15 g	252	60
HORLICKS	25 g	386	92
JARRAH			
chocolatte	11 g	180	43
MILO	20 g	350	84
malt	25 g	450	107

	PORTION SIZE	KJ	CAL
NESQUIK			
chocolate	12 g	210	50
banana; strawberry	10 g	205	49
OVALTINE	15 g	225	54

non-dairy drinks
See also **Milk, Cheese, Yoghurt**

rice milk

FREEDOM FOODS...so natural			
chocolate	250 ml	598	143

soy milk

SANITARIUM			
bliss...chocolate	250 ml	625	149
soyaccino	250 ml	600	143

yoghurt drinks

BULLA...fruit'n yoghurt			
apple	100 g	374	89
apricot; fruit salad	100 g	339	81
raspberry; strawberry	100 g	346	82
JALNA			
strawberry...low fat	100 ml	366	87
vitalize...breakfast; immune	100 ml	366	87
YAKULT			
light	65 ml	149	35
original	65 ml	218	52

Fruit

One of the best snacks you can ever have is a piece of fruit. Fruit is inexpensive, healthy and a great alternative if you have a sweet tooth. It's also convenient. Think of an apple – it even comes with its own wrapper that you can eat! Chuck one in your bag before leaving the house and you have the perfect snack. I prefer my clients to eat a piece of fruit rather than drink fruit juice as it's lower in calories and you get the added benefit of fibre for your intestinal health. I recommend several serves of fruit a day. One serve could be a medium-sized apple, two apricots, or ten strawberries. As always, though, you can have too much of a good thing: too much fruit can hinder your weight management, often because of the levels of natural sugars fruit contains. Tropical fruits like mango and pawpaw tend to be high in calories, whereas berries are very low in calories and high in antioxidants, which is why I love them!

	PORTION SIZE	KJ	CAL
fresh fruit			
apples			
fresh			
Delicious	100 g	211	50
Golden Delicious	100 g	167	40
Granny Smith	100 g	159	38
Jonathan	100 g	188	45
baked; stewed			
with sugar	100 g	345	82
without sugar	100 g	135	32
apricots			
fresh	100 g	171	41
stewed			
with sugar	100 g	350	84
without sugar	100 g	90	22
bananas			
common variety	100 g	378	90
lady finger; sugar	100 g	442	105
blackberries			
fresh	100 g	245	59
stewed			
with sugar	100 g	255	61
without sugar	100 g	125	30
blackcurrants	100 g	245	59
blueberries	100 g	197	47

	PORTION SIZE	KJ	CAL
breadfruit	100 g	445	106
Cape gooseberry	100 g	200	48
cherries			
fresh	100 g	250	60
stewed…no sugar, inc. stones	100 g	140	33
cranberries	100 g	195	47
cumquats	100 g	275	66
custard apple	100 g	326	78
dates	100 g	1055	252
figs	100 g	195	47
gooseberries			
fresh	100 g	180	43
stewed…with sugar	100 g	215	51
grapefruit	100 g	138	33
grapes			
black muscatel	100 g	278	67
Cornichon	100 g	233	55
green/ruby sultana	100 g	250	60
Waltham Cross	100 g	250	60
guavas (flesh, skin + seeds)	100 g	144	34
jackfruit (flesh only)	100 g	347	83
kiwifruit	100 g	164	39
lemons	100 g	95	23
limes	100 g	90	22
loganberries	100 g	217	52
lychees	100 g	296	71

	PORTION SIZE	KJ	CAL
mandarins	100 g	191	46
mangoes	100 g	230	55
melons			
bitter melon	100 g	20	5
canteloupe/rockmelon	100 g	91	22
hairy melon	100 g	46	11
honeydew	100 g	130	31
watermelon	100 g	95	22
mulberries	100 g	139	33
nectarines	100 g	184	44
oranges			
navel	100 g	124	30
Valencia	100 g	109	26
passionfruit	100 g	304	73
pawpaw	100 g	142	34
peaches			
fresh	100 g	195	47
stewed			
with sugar	100 g	395	94
without sugar	100 g	335	80
pears			
Bartlett; Bon Chretien	100 g	177	42
brown skin	100 g	203	49
Packhams Triumph	100 g	198	47
yellow-green skin	100 g	190	45
stewed			

	PORTION SIZE	KJ	CAL
with sugar	100 g	385	92
without sugar	100 g	135	32
pepino	100 g	100	24
persimmon	100 g	298	71
pineapple	100 g	178	43
plums			
red-fleshed; damson	100 g	156	37
yellow-fleshed	100 g	121	28
stewed			
with sugar	100 g	295	71
without sugar	100 g	135	32
pomegranates	100 g	300	72
prickly pear	100 g	204	49
quinces			
fresh, 1 av.	100 g	242	58
stewed with sugar	100 g	350	84
rambutan	100 g	312	75
raspberries			
fresh	100 g	240	57
stewed			
with sugar	100 g	290	69
without sugar	100 g	200	48
redcurrants	100 g	215	51
rhubarb			
stewed			
with sugar	100 g	270	65

	PORTION SIZE	KJ	CAL
without sugar	100 g	25	6
starfruit	100 g	128	31
strawberries	100 g	108	26
sultanas	100 g	1175	281
tamarillo	100 g	150	36
tamarind	100 g	1000	239
tangelo	100 g	172	41
youngberries	100 g	245	59

canned, frozen & dried fruit

apples

	PORTION SIZE	KJ	CAL
canned...av. all brands			
sweetened	100 g	320	76
unsweetened	100 g	175	42
ARDMONA...pie apples...sliced	100 g	190	45

apricots

	PORTION SIZE	KJ	CAL
canned in pear juice...av. all brands			
3 halves + 35 ml juice	85 g	150	36
3 halves in syrup...drained	50 g	105	25
dried	100 g	1125	275
GOULBURN VALLEY...in fruit juice	100 g	277	66
SPC...in juice	100 g	277	66
WEIGHT WATCHERS...artific. sweet	100 g	134	26

blackberries

	PORTION SIZE	KJ	CAL
canned...in syrup	100 g	435	104

blueberries

	PORTION SIZE	**KJ**	**CAL**
frozen			
CREATIVE GOURMET	100 g	215	51
MCCAINS	100 g	236	56
SARA LEE	100 g	262	63
in syrup			
WOOLWORTHS SELECT	100 g	355	85
breadfruit			
canned...drained	100 g	275	66
cherries			
canned...black...in syrup			
JOHN WEST	100 g	371	89
WOOLWORTHS SELECT	100 g	355	85
frozen...CREATIVE GOURMET	100 g	410	98
glacé	100 g	1420	339
sour...pitted	100 g	319	76
cumquats			
canned	100 g	575	137
currants			
dried	100 g	1145	274
dates			
dried...pitted	100 g	1143	271
figs			
dried	100 g	1130	270
glacé	100 g	1250	299
fruit mince			
ROBERTSON'S...traditional	100 g	1178	281

	PORTION SIZE	KJ	CAL
fruit salad			
GOLDEN CIRCLE...in natural juice	100 g	235	56
GOULBURN VALLEY			
in juice	100 g	223	53
snack pack	140 g	238	57
WEIGHT WATCHERS...artific. sweet	100 g	145	35
gooseberries			
canned...av. all brands			
sweetened	100 g	375	90
unsweetened	100 g	110	26
guavas			
canned...in syrup	100 g	255	61
kiwifruit			
canned...in syrup	100 g	340	81
loquats			
canned	100 g	350	84
lychees			
canned...ADMIRAL	100 g	366	87
mandarins			
canned...ADMIRAL	100 g	257	61
mangoes			
canned			
ADMIRAL			
sliced...natural juice	100 g	266	64
GREAT LAKES			
in light syrup	100 g	266	64

	PORTION SIZE	KJ	CAL
mixed berries			
CREATIVE GOURMET...frozen			
forest fruits	100 g	270	64
mixed berries; summer fruits	100 g	240	57
mixed peel			
candied	100 g	1325	317
papaya			
SPC...spears in juice	100 g	191	46
passionfruit			
ADMIRAL...in syrup	100 g	424	101
JOHN WEST...pulp	100 g	464	111
pawpaw			
canned	100 g	275	65
peaches			
canned			
artific. sweet + 40 ml liquid	250 g	263	63
drained	210 g	220	53
in syrup + 25 ml syrup	65 g	140	33
drained	40 g	85	20
GOULBURN VALLEY...snack pack, diced	140 g	238	57
SPC...in juice	100 g	250	60
WEIGHT WATCHERS...artific. sweet	100 g	105	25
pears			
canned			
artific. sweet + 40 ml liquid	95 g	105	25
drained	55 g	60	14

	PORTION SIZE	KJ	CAL
in pear juice … drained	55 g	100	24
in syrup … drained	55 g	135	32
GOULBURN VALLEY			
in juice	100 g	228	54
snack pack (diced)	140 g	236	56
SPC			
in juice	100 g	274	65
in lite juice	100 g	190	45
pineapple			
canned			
drained	200 g	700	167
in heavy syrup	270 g	965	231
in pineapple juice … drained	40 g	75	18
glacé	42 g	555	133
GOLDEN CIRCLE			
crush; pieces; slices; thins … in juice	100 g	240	57
crush; pieces; slices; thins … in syrup	100 g	336	80
plums			
GOULBURN VALLEY … whole in juice	100 g	271	65
prunes			
dried	100 g	1065	255
stewed without sugar	100 g	500	120
SPC … d'agen … in syrup	90 g	627	150
quinces			
canned	100 g	350	84
raisins	100 g	1167	280

	PORTION SIZE	KJ	CAL
raspberries			
canned			
in juice	100 g	200	48
in syrup	100 g	425	102
frozen			
CREATIVE GOURMET	100 g	220	52
McCAINS	100 g	245	58
SARA LEE	100 g	180	43
strawberries			
canned...av. all brands			
sweetened	100 g	245	59
unsweetened	100 g	90	22
frozen...whole...sweetened	100 g	475	114

Vegetables

Vegetables are the KING of all the food groups. You should be aiming for at least five serves of vegetables a day, and you'll be blown away by how low the calorie count is on these guys and just how many of them you can eat. I try to include them in all my meals and even use them in a lot for my snacks (having some cut-up veggies in a zip-top bag in the fridge means you always have a healthy snack ready to go). For dinner, the main part of my meals is the vegetables and the meat is simply the garnish. About three-quarters of your plate should be vegetables. Aim to mix up your colours (the nutrients that give veggies their colour are really good for you), but always have plenty of green. Besides the obvious benefit of low calories, your body will come alive with the extra nutrients. Whenever possible, use vegetables that are in season. This is when they are at their tastiest and most nutritious; it's also when they are cheapest. Frozen vegetables are great to have in the freezer, as they are frozen just after harvest, retaining all the goodness.

	PORTION SIZE	KJ	CAL

fresh vegetables

See also **Herbs, Spices, Seasonings**

	PORTION SIZE	KJ	CAL
alfalfa sprouts	100 g	91	22
artichoke, globe			
steamed...inner leaves + base	100 g	87	21
artichoke, Jerusalem			
steamed...peeled	100 g	103	24
asparagus			
steamed	100 g	105	25
avocado	100 g	862	206
bamboo shoots	100 g	155	28
bean sprouts	100 g	84	20
beans, broad			
raw...fresh	100 g	230	55
steamed	100 g	247	59
beans, butter			
raw...fresh	100 g	100	24
steamed	100 g	103	24
beans, green			
raw	100 g	81	20
steamed	100 g	76	19
beans, mung			
raw...fresh	100 g	980	234
sprouts	100 g	84	20

	PORTION SIZE	KJ	CAL
beans, purple			
raw...fresh	100 g	159	38
steamed	100 g	121	29
beans, soy			
raw...fresh	100 g	560	134
beetroot			
boiled...flesh only	100 g	201	48
bok choy	100 g	54	13
broccoli			
boiled; raw	100 g	100	24
Chinese...raw	100 g	150	36
broccolini	100 g	179	43
brussels sprouts			
boiled	100 g	105	25
cabbage See also bok choy, choy sum, wombok, gai choy (in this section)			
common; savoy; white			
boiled	100 g	93	22
raw	100 g	90	22
red			
boiled	100 g	127	30
raw	100 g	122	29
capsicum			
green			
boiled	100 g	76	18
raw	100 g	92	22

	PORTION SIZE	**KJ**	**CAL**
red			
boiled	100 g	117	28
raw	100 g	106	25
carrots			
baby			
boiled; raw...peeled	100 g	132	32
mature			
boiled...peeled	100 g	141	34
raw...peeled	100 g	99	23
cassava			
boiled...peeled	100 g	632	151
cauliflower			
steamed/raw	100 g	99	24
celeriac			
raw...peeled	100 g	159	38
steamed...peeled	100 g	171	41
celery			
raw	100 g	65	15
steamed	100 g	56	14
chicory			
raw	100 g	67	16
steamed	100 g	79	19
chillies See **Herbs, Spices, Seasonings**			
chokoes			
boiled...peeled	100 g	103	25
choy sum (flower cabbage)	100 g	50	13

	PORTION SIZE	KJ	CAL
coriander See **Herbs, Spices, Seasonings**			
corn			
steamed	100 g	438	105
courgettes See zucchini (in this section)			
cucumber			
apple...raw...unpeeled	100 g	42	10
Lebanese...raw...unpeeled	100 g	51	12
telegraph...raw...unpeeled	100 g	41	10
eggplant			
baked	100 g	260	62
steamed	100 g	82	19
endive	100 g	58	14
fennel			
steamed; raw	100 g	92	22
gai choy (mustard cabbage)	100 g	109	26
garlic See **Herbs, Spices, Seasonings**			
ginger See **Herbs, Spices, Seasonings**			
horseradish See **Herbs, Spices, Seasonings**			
kale			
raw	100 g	180	43
steamed	100 g	160	38
kohlrabi			
raw...peeled	100 g	163	39
boiled...peeled	100 g	170	41
leeks			
raw	100 g	125	30

	PORTION SIZE	KJ	CAL
steamed	100 g	130	31
lettuce			
butter	100 g	67	46
common	100 g	40	10
cos	100 g	80	19
mignonette	100 g	64	15
radicchio	100 g	30	8
marrow, vegetable			
boiled...peeled	100 g	80	19
raw...peeled	100 g	84	20
mushrooms			
oyster	100 g	85	20
button	100 g	100	24
sautéed in butter	100 g	460	110
okra			
boiled	100 g	95	23
onions			
fried...av. all varieties	100 g	1425	341
onions, brown			
raw	100 g	110	26
boiled	100 g	114	27
onions, spring			
raw	100 g	127	30
onions, white			
raw	100 g	112	26
boiled	100 g	121	28

	PORTION SIZE	KJ	CAL
peas, green			
fresh	100 g	225	60
steamed	100 g	203	48
peas, snow/sugar			
steamed/raw	100 g	151	36
parsley See **Herbs, Spices, Seasonings**			
parsnip			
steamed	100 g	259	62
plantain			
boiled	100 g	520	124
green...raw	100 g	475	114
ripe...fried	100 g	1125	269
potatoes			
baked			
flesh only (not skin)	100 g	305	73
in jacket	100 g	283	67
topped with cheese & bacon	100 g	630	151
topped with sour cream & chives	100 g	545	130
mashed...+ milk + butter	100 g	443	106
new			
peeled...steamed	100 g	267	63
other varieties...peeled			
boiled	100 g	252	60
roasted	100 g	447	107
pumpkin			
butternut			

	PORTION SIZE	KJ	CAL
mashed	100 g	205	49
steamed	100 g	194	46
golden nugget…boiled	100 g	127	30
Queensland blue…boiled	100 g	216	52
radish			
oriental…raw	100 g	73	18
red…raw	100 g	62	15
white…raw	100 g	86	21
shallots			
raw	100 g	104	25
steamed	100 g	50	10
silverbeet			
raw	100 g	55	16
steamed	100 g	82	20
spinach			
Chinese; common			
raw	100 g	101	24
steamed	100 g	80	19
squash, button			
raw	100 g	106	25
steamed	100 g	126	30
squash, scaloppini			
raw	100 g	83	20
steamed	100 g	100	24
squash, winter			
raw	100 g	190	45

	PORTION SIZE	KJ	CAL
steamed	100 g	165	39
swede			
boiled	100 g	81	19
sweet potato			
orange flesh...boiled	100 g	272	65
white flesh...boiled	100 g	321	76
sweetcorn See corn (in this section)			
taro			
boiled	100 g	504	121
tomatoes			
raw	100 g	74	18
fried	100 g	290	69
tomatoes, cherry	100 g	73	18
tomatoes, roma	100 g	60	15
turnip, white			
boiled	100 g	101	24
vegetable curry			
homemade	100 g	755	180
wakame (seaweed)	10 g	130	31
watercress			
raw	100 g	110	26
witlof See chicory (in this section)			
wombok (Chinese cabbage)	100 g	68	16
zucchini			
green-skinned			
raw	100 g	61	15

	PORTION SIZE	KJ	CAL
steamed	100 g	64	15
golden			
raw	100 g	67	16
steamed	100 g	77	19

canned, frozen & pickled vegetables

artichoke, globe

artichoke hearts...av. all brands	100 g	155	37
ALWAYS FRESH			
marinated artichoke hearts	100 g	815	195

asparagus

canned			
EDGELL...av. all varieties	100 g	78	18
JOHN WEST			
cuts and tips	100 g	100	24
spears	100 g	121	29
marinated...av. all brands	100 g	125	30

baked beans

HEINZ			
in tomato sauce	100 g	380	91
SPC			
ham	100 g	436	104
rich tomato	100 g	369	88

beans, broad

frozen			
LOGAN FARM	100 g	196	46

	PORTION SIZE	KJ	CAL
HEINZ	100 g	225	54
beans, butter			
EDGELL...frozen	100 g	505	121
beans, dried			
blackeye; borlotti; cannellini; haricot;			
red kidney; lima...boiled...av. all brands	100 g	400	95
beans, green			
canned...drained	100 g	100	24
BIRDS EYE...sliced	100 g	117	28
EDGELL...canned	100 g	149	36
McCAIN...frozen...sliced	100 g	163	39
beans, mixed			
EDGELL...four-bean mix	100 g	497	119
beans, mung			
cooked (dahl)	100 g	350	84
dried...raw	100 g	1430	342
sprouts	100 g	145	35
canned	100 g	40	10
beans, red kidney			
canned...drained...av. all brands	100 g	375	90
EDGELL	100 g	499	119
OLD EL PASO			
mexe	100 g	299	71
refried	100 g	318	76
WOOLWORTHS HOME BRAND	100 g	307	73
beans, soy			

	PORTION SIZE	KJ	CAL
boiled...dried	100 g	545	130
canned...drained	100 g	385	92
beetroot			
canned			
EDGELL...sliced	100 g	223	53
GOLDEN CIRCLE...drained...whole baby	100 g	253	61
broccoli			
frozen			
BIRDS EYE...florets	100 g	88	21
McCAIN	100 g	100	24
brussels sprouts			
BIRDS EYE...frozen	100 g	108	26
cabbage			
EDGELL...canned...sauerkraut	100 g	67	16
capers			
av. commercial brands	100 g	122	29
capsicum			
EDGELL...canned	100 g	135	32
carrots			
baby			
McCAIN...frozen	100 g	145	35
mature			
canned	100 g	135	32
BIRDS EYE...julienne	100 g	134	32
cauliflower			
canned	100 g	100	24

	PORTION SIZE	KJ	CAL
frozen			
BIRDS EYE	100 g	97	23
McCAIN	100 g	93	22
champignons			
ALWAYS FRESH...pieces and stems; whole	100 g	139	33
chick peas See peas, chick (in this section)			
corn			
canned			
drained...baby	100 g	90	22
EDGELL			
creamed	100 g	356	85
kernels	100 g	486	116
GOLDEN CIRCLE			
creamed	100 g	284	68
kernels, drained	100 g	306	73
frozen			
BIRDS EYE			
fritters...oven bake	56 g	490	117
kernels	100 g	476	114
LOGAN FARM...extra-juicy cobs	100 g	345	82
McCAIN...cobettes	100 g	485	116
cucumber			
GOLDEN CIRCLE...canned, drained	100 g	371	89
dill cucumber See gherkins (in this section)			
dolmades See vine leaves...stuffed (in this section)			
eggplant...pickled ... grilled			

	PORTION SIZE	KJ	CAL
ALWAYS FRESH	100 g	862	206
frijoles (pinto beans)			
with cheese	100 g	566	135
gherkins	100 g	131	64
lentils			
boiled (dahl)	100 g	295	71
dried	100 g	1405	336
EDGELL...brown...canned	100 g	383	91
mushrooms			
canned			
straw...drained	100 g	125	30
EDGELL...sliced in butter sauce	100 g	128	31
SPC...in butter sauce	100 g	132	32
dried	100 g	1150	275
marinated...ALWAYS FRESH	100 g	252	60
olives			
black olives	20 g	166	39
green olives	20 g	107	26
ALWAYS FRESH			
anchovy stuffed	20 g	94	22
deli style...Greek jumbo	20 g	189	45
deli style...Queen olives	20 g	55	13
kalamata	20 g	156	37
onions			
BIRDS EYE...frozen...chopped	100 g	129	31
ALWAYS FRESH...pickled	100 g	128	64

	PORTION SIZE	KJ	CAL
balsamic marinated	100 g	240	57
cocktail…white	100 g	367	88
standard	100 g	260	62
peas, chick			
boiled	100 g	685	164
cooked (dahl)	100 g	610	146
dry seed	100 g	1315	314
BIO NATURE…organic	100 g	568	135
EDGELL	100 g	532	127
peas, green			
canned			
drained	100 g	251	60
BIRDS EYE…baby	100 g	243	58
HEINZ…green	100 g	360	86
EDGELL			
baby	100 g	338	81
garden	100 g	418	100
GOLDEN CIRCLE…drained	100 g	317	75
frozen			
boiled	100 g	209	50
LOGAN FARM…garden	100 g	273	65
McCAIN…baby	100 g	399	95
split			
boiled	100 g	244	59
dried	100 g	1455	348

	PORTION SIZE	KJ	CAL
pimientos			
canned...solid + liquid	100 g	115	27
potatoes			
canned			
new...drained	100 g	237	57
EDGELL...tiny taters	100 g	272	65
dehydrated			
made up...3 parts water, 1 part whole milk	100 g	380	91
DEB...plain...made up	100 g	333	79
EDGELL...instant mash...made up	100 g	305	73
frozen			
BIRDS EYE			
hash browns	100 g	733	175
potato gems original	100 g	639	153
potato chips			
homemade	100 g	800	191
BIRDS EYE			
oven bake...chunky cut	100 g	441	105
golden crunch chips	100 g	526	126
oven bake chips...French fries	100 g	633	151
LOGAN FARM			
guilt-free oven fries	100 g	650	155
McCAIN			
chunky cut	100 g	517	124
healthy choice	100 g	531	127
straight cut	100 g	519	124

	PORTION SIZE	KJ	CAL
potato wedges			
McCAIN...healthy choice	100 g	519	124
salads			
bean salad	100 g	580	141
coleslaw	100 g	451	109
potato salad	100 g	397	95
rice	100 g	558	133
tabouli	100 g	610	146
waldorf	100 g	521	125
sauerkraut			
EDGELL...canned	100 g	67	16
spinach			
LOGAN FARM...frozen	100 g	102	24
tomatoes			
ALDI...just organic	100 g	94	22
ARDMONA...whole peeled...no added salt	100 g	102	24
EDGELL...supreme	100 g	195	46
tomatoes, sundried			
ALWAYS FRESH...strips	22 g	206	49
vegetables, mixed			
BIRDS EYE...steam fresh			
carrot, cauliflower, broccoli	100 g	116	28
peas, corn, carrot	100 g	266	63
GOLDEN CIRCLE			
corn and peas, drained	100 g	307	73

	PORTION SIZE	KJ	CAL
McCAIN...gourmet creations			
Bombay mix	100 g	322	77
Mediterranean vegetables	100 g	340	87
vine leaves			
raw	100 g	65	16
stuffed	100 g	455	109
vegetarian	100 g	715	171
water chestnuts			
VALCOM	100 g	247	59

soy, tofu & other meat substitutes

	PORTION SIZE	KJ	CAL
soya burgers			
with tempeh	100 g	860	205
tempeh	100 g	659	157
tofu			
canned...fried	100 g	1265	302
SOYCO TOFU			
Chinese honey soy	100 g	714	171
Japanese; Thai	100 g	732	175
meat substitutes			
SANITARIUM			
casserole mince	138 g	497	119
country hot pot	138 g	414	99
nut meat	85 g	748	179
vegie delights			
classic hot dogs	100 g	710	170

	PORTION SIZE	KJ	CAL
lentil patties	75 g	473	113
not burgers	94 g	827	198
rashers...bacon style	100 g	980	234
traditional sausages...vegie	100 g	820	196
traditional soy sausages...BBQ	100 g	720	172
vegie roast	100 g	880	210
bean meals, canned			
SPC...bean cuisine			
mild chilli	100 g	322	77
Moroccan	100 g	326	78
rich Italian	100 g	326	78
spicy Mexican	100 g	314	75
vegekabana			
with tempeh	16 g	155	37

Bread

Carbohydrates have been given a bad rap over the years, and bread is loaded with carbs. But we need carbohydrates in our diet; they give us energy and stop us getting tired and cranky. They also help us to feel full, so I recommend choosing low-GI, wholegrain and unrefined breads. These types have more nutrients and fibre than the processed, white varieties, while bread containing seeds gives your body the vital minerals of those seeds, alongside the benefits of the bread itself. I often have a slice of soy & linseed with my breakfast or a chicken salad multigrain sandwich for lunch. But remember, carbs give you energy for your daily activities – they're not a great idea at night (unless you're a shift worker, of course!). And avoid high-calorie mayonnaises and sandwich spreads; they cause your calorie count to shoot up.

	PORTION SIZE	KJ	CAL
loaves (av. 2 slices)			
mixed grain	120 g	540	128
pumpernickel	120 g	920	220
rye			
dark	100 g	850	204
light	74 g	750	179
Vienna	60 g	620	148
ALDI			
be light			
four grains	63 g	498	119
pumpernickel	56 g	470	112
rye	63 g	508	121
sunflower seed	63 g	558	132
ALPINE			
multigrain	80 g	856	204
sourdough	60 g	1070	255
spelt	80 g	816	196
wholemeal	80 g	709	188
ATLANTIC BAKERY			
light rye	48 g	470	112
special rye	64 g	510	122
BURGEN			
mixed grain	83 g	788	188
rye	83 g	804	192
BUTTERCUP			

	PORTION SIZE	KJ	CAL
country split			
white	47 g	490	117
wholemeal	47 g	470	112
COUNTRY LIFE BAKERY			
country grain	65 g	757	181
gluten-free multigrain	73 g	745	178
organic rye	82 g	781	187
EDWARDS			
sourdough			
yeast-free organic rye	72 g	766	183
HELGA'S			
light rye	68 g	700	167
mixed grain with oats	85 g	906	216
soy & linseed	85 g	915	219
traditional			
white	83 g	868	207
wholemeal	83 g	798	191
MOLENBERG			
swiss bake			
original sandwich	70 g	714	170
soy & linseed	70 g	814	194
NOBLE RISE			
rye; spelt	84 g	852	203
soy & linseed	95 g	1055	252
traditional white with oats	84 g	814	194
wholemeal	95 g	872	208

	PORTION SIZE	KJ	CAL
wholemeal; grain	95 g	942	225
SCHWOBS SWISS			
fruit muesli blend	82 g	790	189
kibbled rye	82 g	781	187
light rye	66 g	598	143
multigrain	66 g	663	158
soy & linseed	82 g	757	181
TIP TOP			
cafe extra thick raisin toast	65 g	981	234
corn	79 g	877	210
pumpkin seed	74 g	824	197
soy & linseed	79 g	830	198
sunblest...thick			
multigrain	60 g	640	153
white	68 g	710	170
wholemeal	68 g	714	171
sunflower, oats & honey	74 g	813	194
white plus omega 3	74 g	763	182
wholemeal	79 g	815	195

flat breads

	PORTION SIZE	KJ	CAL
BAZAAR			
pide	100 g	997	238
wholemeal lavash	56 g	740	176
wholemeal pita	67 g	728	174

	PORTION SIZE	KJ	CAL
Lebanese pocket (24 cm)			
white	110 g	1234	295
wholemeal	110 g	1086	260
matzo	30 g	490	117
MOUNTAIN BREAD			
pocket			
white; wholemeal	45 g	510	122
roti			
classic Indian	47 g	625	149
sorj	100 g	1205	288
wraps			
corn; oat	25 g	295	70
wholewheat; white; rye; rice; barley	25 g	300	71
TAJ ROTI CO.			
chapati			
garlic	47 g	630	150
plain	47 g	625	149

buns, English muffins, rolls, sticks

buns

brioche	100 g	1720	411
cinnamon	55 g	680	163
fruit…iced	76 g	940	225
hot cross	90 g	915	219

	PORTION SIZE	KJ	CAL
croissants See **Sweet Pies & Pastries**			
crumpets			
GOLDEN			
breaks	71 g	492	117
crumpet toast	88 g	807	192
golden	50 g	347	83
muffins, English			
MIGHTY SOFT			
English standard	63 g	620	148
fruit n' spice	64 g	630	150
TIP TOP			
9 grain; spicy fruit	67 g	645	154
English	67 g	652	156
rolls			
bap; hamburger	65 g	645	154
cheese	65 g	710	170
dinner	30 g	300	72
horseshoe; knot; mixed-grain; torpedo	60 g	595	142
TIP TOP			
hamburger	87 g	987	236
hot dog	75 g	824	197
sticks			
French; wholemeal	20 g	200	48
grissini	20 g	300	72

	PORTION SIZE	KJ	CAL
garlic bread			
LA FAMIGLIA…homestyle	33 g	432	103

bread mixes, breadcrumbs, yeast

bread mixes

BASCO…gluten-free	35 g	347	83
LAUCKE			
barossa sourdough rye	100 g	932	223
crusty white	100 g	954	228
german grain	100 g	943	225
supersoft white	100 g	996	238
TIP TOP KITCHEN COLLECTION			
grain	100 g	1085	260
soy & linseed	100 g	1060	255
white	100 g	989	238
wholemeal	100 g	959	230
breadcrumbs			
commercial…dried	12 g	178	42
yeast			
dried			
bakers	10 g	127	30
brewers	10 g	121	29
fresh compressed…bakers	10 g	36	9
LOWAN…dried	6 g	77	18
TANDACO…dried	7 g	97	23

Breakfast cereals

Always check the calorie content label of cereals. There are a lot of high-calorie, highly processed cereals out there with not that much nutritional value, and these are the ones we often give to our children! They also tend to have higher levels of sugar. Some cereals offer good low-GI carbohydrates and fibre, but you need to choose the least refined ones. Also, be conscious of your portion sizes and always measure your brekkie with a measuring cup. That way you can stay in control of your calorie intake. If it's a lighter cereal I'll have a cup, if it's a denser cereal (e.g. oats) then just half a cup. Add a few chopped berries to your cereal for a burst of sweetness and try to use skim milk. Porridge makes a good start to the day as it slowly releases its energy, keeping you feeling full until lunchtime and so less likely to snack. The one thing I have to add is – eat brekkie! Skipping meals is not a good idea, either for a healthy diet or losing weight. It's not about under-eating; it's about optimum eating.

	PORTION SIZE	KJ	CAL

plain cereals

	PORTION SIZE	KJ	CAL
ABUNDANT EARTH (organic puffed)			
corn	30 g	483	116
kamut	30 g	393	94
millet	30 g	450	108
rice	30 g	483	116
ALDI			
be light...all varieties	30 g	480	114
FREEDOM FOODS (gluten free)			
corn flakes	45 g	815	195
rice flakes	45 g	743	177
rice puffs	45 g	477	114
KELLOGG'S			
all bran	45 g	620	148
all bran...tropical	45 g	638	152
cornflakes	30 g	475	113
guardian	30 g	432	103
mini-wheats 5 grains	40 g	600	143
rice bubbles	30 g	480	115
special K	30 g	472	113
sultana bran	30 g	640	153
ORGRAN			
supergrains...puffed	30 g	510	122
SANITARIUM			
lite 'n tasty...av. all flavours	30 g	465	111

	PORTION SIZE	KJ	CAL
puffed wheat	30 g	465	111
weet-bix	30 g	447	107
weet-bix hi-bran	40 g	596	142
weet-bix multigrain	48 g	782	187
UNCLE TOBY'S			
bran plus	45 g	540	129
oat flakes	30 g	500	119
vita brits…organic; original	33 g	500	119
weeties	30 g	460	110
VOGELS			
soy & linseed ultra bran	45 g	595	142
WOOLWORTHS HOME BRAND			
processed bran	35 g	473	113
unprocessed bran	30 g	324	77

mixed cereals with fruit/nuts

	PORTION SIZE	KJ	CAL
KELLOGG'S			
crunchy nut cornflakes	30 g	497	119
just right	45 g	670	160
sustain	45 g	710	169
UNCLE TOBY'S			
healthwise			
for bowel and digestive system	45 g	700	167
for heart and circulatory system	45 g	720	172
for women 40+	45 g	690	165
fruity bites	35 g	540	129

	PORTION SIZE	KJ	CAL
vita weeties	45 g	460	110

muesli

ABUNDANT EARTH

organic bircher...orchard fruits & almond	45 g	626	149

ARNOLD'S FARM

farmhouse	30 g	510	130
full o' fruit	30 g	543	121
strawberry & yoghurt	30 g	483	165
wild berry	30 g	470	118

CARMANS

classic (fruit)	45 g	873	208
deluxe (nuts)	45 g	633	151
natural (untoasted)	45 g	765	183
original	45 g	878	209

KELLOGG'S

komplete...oven baked	45 g	730	174

LOWAN WHOLE FOODS

apricot & almond	45 g	817	195
Australian gold...tropical fruit	45 g	741	177
Swiss	45 g	718	171

MORNING SUN

apricot almond	45 g	675	161
peach & pecan	45 g	700	167

NU-VIT

low-fat gluten-free fruity	40 g	600	143

	PORTION SIZE	KJ	CAL
low-fat natural	40 g	549	131
mega high-protein	40 g	613	146
UNCLE TOBY'S			
apple & cranberry	60 g	940	224
natural	60 g	880	210
Swiss	60 g	920	219
VOGELS			
premium oven crisp	45 g	797	190

porridge

oatmeal; rolled oats			
boiled	100 g	273	65
semolina			
cooked	200 g	260	62
FREEDOM FOODS			
quick oats	30 g	735	175
LOWAN WHOLE FOODS			
rice…with orchard fruits	50 g	731	175
wholegrain rolled oats	30 g	465	111
UNCLE TOBY'S			
oats…quick; traditional	30 g	480	115
oats temptations			
sultanas, apple & honey	40 g	630	150
wild berry basket	35 g	550	131
quick oats satchets…original	34 g	540	129
WOOLWORTHS HOME BRAND …rolled oats	30 g	510	122

	PORTION SIZE	**KJ**	**CAL**

other cereals

KELLOGG'S

coco pops	30 g	480	115
crispix...honey	30 g	488	117
froot loops	30 g	490	117
frosties	30 g	484	116
nutrigrain	30 g	480	115

SANITARIUM

granola clusters...vanilla & almond	50 g	880	210

breakfast bars

ARNOLD'S FARM

almond & sesame	40 g	633	151

FREEDOM FOODS

hi-lite

muesli	35 g	616	147
regular; super berry	35 g	420	100

SANITARIUM

weetbix...fruity apricot; wild berry	45 g	635	152

Flour, pasta, noodles, rice, grains

When it comes to flour, pasta, noodles, rice and grains, always go for the least processed product you can. Choose wholegrain, unprocessed flour and pasta, bulghur wheat or barley, basmati or brown rice. These are great low-GI choices that offer the added benefit of insoluble fibre (which helps keep your digestive system in good shape). Buckwheat pasta is also a good addition to your diet as it is one of the few types that contain protein, as well as being high in fibre. Fibre is also important as it helps fill us up – perfect if you are looking to lose some weight. Don't be fooled into thinking that these foods are necessarily 'fattening' – it's the overconsumption of poor-quality carbohydrates that leads to weight gain, so reduce your portions. Pasta, rice and noodles are often the base of a dish so, even though you are choosing a healthier base, make sure what you add to it doesn't up your calorie count excessively. Choose tomato sauces for pasta rather than creamy ones, serve rice with a stir-fry rather than a rich curry, and toss noodles through a salad for a filling, healthy lunch.

	PORTION SIZE	KJ	CAL

flour

	PORTION SIZE	KJ	CAL
arrowroot	10 g	156	37
buckwheat...**LOWAN WHOLE FOODS**	100 g	1523	363
carob	100 g	956	229
chickpea	100 g	1406	336
corn; maize...av. all brands	100 g	1454	348
millet...**LOTUS**	100 g	1582	378
potato	100 g	2070	495
quinoa...**LOTUS**	100 g	1586	379
rice...**MACRO**...brown	100 g	1347	322
self-raising flour See wheat flour (in this section)			
soy			
low-fat	100 g	1485	355
MACRO	100 g	1851	442
tapioca	100 g	1496	358

wheat flour

	PORTION SIZE	KJ	CAL
fortified	100 g	1525	364
plain			
white	100 g	1475	353
white spelt...**MACRO**	100 g	1623	388
wholemeal	100 g	1170	280
wholemeal spelt...**MACRO**	100 g	1604	383
self-raising			
white	100 g	1410	337
wholemeal	100 g	1111	266

	PORTION SIZE	KJ	CAL
pasta			
durum wheat (cooked)			
egg; spinach	100 g	545	130
plain	100 g	497	119
wholemeal	100 g	546	130
LATINA			
beef ravioli	100 g	830	198
egg fettuccine	100 g	606	144
pappardelle	100 g	818	195
ricotta spinach agnolotti	100 g	830	198
roasted veg ravioli	100 g	758	181
SAN REMO...all varieties	100 g	1518	363
corn			
ORGRAN...rice & corn...all varieties	100 g	1380	327
gnocchi			
LATINA...potato	100 g	861	206
lasagne			
LATINA...instant sheets	100 g	806	192
ORGRAN...rice & corn mini	100 g	1380	330
SARA LEE (frozen)			
beef lasagne	100 g	790	165
spaghetti			
with marinara sauce	100 g	545	130
with napoletana sauce	100 g	485	116

	PORTION SIZE	KJ	CAL

noodles

HAKUBAKU...organic			
ramen	100 g	1450	346
soba	100 g	1485	355
udon	100 g	1424	340
KAN TONG...shelf fresh			
hokkien	100 g	672	161
udon	100 g	712	170
PUREHARVEST...brown rice ramen... with seasoning	100 g	1458	348
WOKKA...shelf fresh			
Singapore-style	100 g	534	128
thin egg	100 g	546	130
thin hokkien	100 g	522	125
udon	100 g	533	132

rice

basmati	100 g	550	134
brown	100 g	630	150
fried rice	100 g	929	222
sushi rice, cooked	100 g	544	130
rice cakes See **Biscuits**			
white	100 g	995	238
wholegrain	100 g	505	121
wild rice...**CAMBRIAN CANADIAN LAKE**...raw	100 g	1525	364

	PORTION SIZE	KJ	CAL
KOALA			
long-grain...raw	100 g	1470	351
long-grain jasmine	100 g	840	200
MAHATMA...natural brown	100 g	640	152
RIVIANA			
arborio	100 g	550	131
basmati; jasmine	100 g	447	107
SUNRICE...raw			
arborio	100 g	1470	352
basmati	100 g	621	148
brown...medium grain	100 g	790	189
koshihikari (Japanese-style sushi rice)	100 g	1440	344
UNCLE BEN'S...organic...white	100 g	1470	352

tacos & tortillas

	PORTION SIZE	KJ	CAL
OLD EL PASO			
taco shells	11 g	230	55
tortillas	40 g	568	135
jumbo tortillas	75 g	1070	254

grains, meals & starches

	PORTION SIZE	KJ	CAL
amaranth	100 g	1554	372
arrowroot	100 g	1445	345
buckwheat...raw	100 g	1520	363
bulgur (bourghul)			
dry	100 g	1250	299

	PORTION SIZE	KJ	CAL
soaked	100 g	636	152
cornmeal	100 g	1530	366
couscous...cooked	100 g	468	112
maize meal			
refined...60%	100 g	1485	355
whole...90%	100 g	1520	363
millet	100 g	1350	323
oatmeal See **Breakfast Cereals**			
pearl barley			
boiled	100 g	450	110
dried...uncooked	100 g	1235	292
polenta...**LOWAN WHOLE FOODS**	100 g	1380	330
quinoa...cooked	100 g	535	128
rye meal	100 g	1400	335
sago...dry	100 g	1500	359
semolina See **Breakfast Cereals**			
soy grits	100 g	1665	400
soy lecithin granules...**LOWAN WHOLE FOODS**	100 g	2100	502
wheat starch	100 g	1455	348
Yorkshire pudding	100 g	900	215

Meat, poultry, deli meats

Protein plays a vital role in our health, but most Australians actually eat too much of it. One serve is only two small lamb chops, but many of us would see that as a snack! Work on between 120 and 150 g of meat per day – that's plenty. And limit red meat to just twice a week, as it is higher in saturated fats than white meat. In fact, why not go vegetarian at least one day a week? It'll do wonders for your health and is better for the environment, as meat production takes a lot more energy than plants. When it comes to meat, as with all food choices, it should be about quality not quantity. Choose meat that looks close to its original state. Organic is best as it has not been adulterated with preservatives or other chemicals, while free range ensures that animal welfare is high. Always cut off the fat/skin and minimise highly processed or deli meats which tend to be higher in salt. Personally, I rate kangaroo – it's environmentally friendly, high in protein, low in fat and inexpensive. Note that portion sizes exclude the bone.

	PORTION SIZE	KJ	CAL

meat

See also **Takeaway Food; Frozen & Convenience Meals**

beef

blade steak... grilled			
lean	100 g	685	164
lean + fat	100 g	740	177
boneless... average cut... cooked			
lean	100 g	766	183
lean + fat	100 g	992	237
brisket, corned... boiled			
lean	100 g	890	212
lean + fat	100 g	1302	428
chuck steak... simmered			
lean	100 g	849	203
lean + fat	100 g	1073	256
fillet steak... grilled			
lean	100 g	745	178
lean + fat	100 g	793	190
mince			
dry fried	100 g	888	212
oxtail... simmered	100 g	1468	351
rib steak (porterhouse)... grilled			
lean	100 g	676	162
lean + fat	100 g	1007	241
rib-eye steak... grilled			

	PORTION SIZE	KJ	CAL
lean	100 g	757	181
lean + fat	100 g	863	206
round steak... grilled			
lean	100 g	617	148
lean + fat	100 g	630	151
rump steak			
fried	100 g	1024	245
grilled			
lean	100 g	740	177
lean + fat	100 g	804	192
silverside... baked			
lean	100 g	665	159
lean + fat	100 g	680	163
silverside, corned... boiled			
lean	100 g	543	130
lean + fat	100 g	852	204
sirloin roast	100 g	1132	271
sirloin steak... grilled			
lean	100 g	676	162
lean + fat	100 g	1007	241
skirt steak... grilled			
lean	100 g	856	205
lean + fat	100 g	922	221
topside roast... baked			
lean	100 g	662	158
lean + fat	100 g	675	161

	PORTION SIZE	KJ	CAL
goat			
meat + skin	100 g	610	146
kangaroo			
fresh	100 g	625	149
lamb			
average cut... cooked			
lean	100 g	766	183
lean + fat	100 g	991	237
breast... rolled... baked	100 g	1210	289
chump chop... grilled			
lean	100 g	1063	254
lean + fat	100 g	1131	271
cutlets... crumbed, fried			
lean	100 g	1435	343
lean + fat	100 g	1945	465
leg... roasted			
lean	100 g	833	199
lean + fat	100 g	841	201
mid-loin chop... grilled			
lean	34 g	250	60
lean + fat	48 g	735	176
mince... simmered	100 g	1265	302
rib-loin cutlet... grilled			
lean	29 g	235	56
lean + fat	39 g	555	133
shank... simmered			

	PORTION SIZE	KJ	CAL
lean	100 g	690	165
lean + fat	100 g	925	221
shoulder... baked			
lean	100 g	714	172
lean + fat	100 g	1188	284
pork			
average cut... cooked			
lean	100 g	710	170
lean + fat	100 g	1252	299
barbecued (Chinese)	100 g	995	238
butterfly steak... grilled			
lean	100 g	675	161
lean + fat	100 g	838	209
forequarter chops... grilled			
lean	100 g	780	186
lean + fat	100 g	1380	330
leg... roasted			
lean	100 g	599	143
lean + fat	100 g	956	229
leg steak... roasted			
lean	100 g	599	143
lean + fat	100 g	956	229
medallion steak... grilled			
lean	100 g	784	188
lean + fat	100 g	1230	294
mid-loin chop... grilled			

	PORTION SIZE	KJ	CAL
lean	100 g	728	174
lean + fat	100 g	1535	367
mince...cooked	100 g	1055	252
trotters and tails...boiled	100 g	1160	277
rabbit			
baked	100 g	855	204
stewed	100 g	785	188
veal			
average cut...cooked			
lean	100 g	623	149
lean + fat	100 g	668	159
forequarter...simmered			
lean	100 g	726	174
lean + fat	100 g	781	187
leg...baked			
lean	100 g	596	142
lean + fat	100 g	600	144
leg steak...fried			
lean	100 g	662	158
lean + fat	100 g	675	161
loin chop...grilled			
lean	100 g	628	150
lean + fat	100 g	730	190
schnitzel...crumbed, fried	100 g	904	216
shank...simmered			
lean	100 g	612	146

	PORTION SIZE	KJ	CAL
lean + fat	100 g	744	178
shoulder steak...grilled			
lean	100 g	620	138
lean + fat	100 g	640	160
venison (deer)			
roasted	100 g	830	198

offal

	PORTION SIZE	KJ	CAL
beef heart...simmered	190 g	1190	284
beef kidney...simmered	100 g	567	136
beef liver...simmered	140 g	1290	308
beef tongue...simmered	100 g	1300	310
chicken liver...floured, fried	100 g	1123	268
haggis...boiled	100 g	1290	308
lamb brains			
crumbed, fried	100 g	1220	292
simmered	100 g	562	135
lamb kidney			
fried	100 g	890	213
simmered	100 g	610	146
lamb liver...fried	100 g	1012	243
lamb tongue			
canned...av. all brands	100 g	810	194
simmered	100 g	1154	276
sweetbreads...raw	100 g	860	206
tripe...raw	100 g	250	60

	PORTION SIZE	KJ	CAL
veal brains			
boiled	100 g	450	108
crumbed, fried	100 g	1220	292
veal liver...grilled	100 g	788	188

poultry

chicken

	PORTION SIZE	KJ	CAL
average cut			
baked			
meat + skin	100 g	1032	246
meat	100 g	782	187
rotisseried			
meat & skin	100 g	1013	242
breast...baked			
meat + skin	100 g	900	215
meat	100 g	637	152
crisp-skin (Chinese)	100 g	860	206
drumsticks...baked			
meat + skin	100 g	960	230
meat	100 g	740	177
leg qtr...rotisseried...meat + skin	100 g	1120	268

duck

	PORTION SIZE	KJ	CAL
roasted	100 g	1310	313

goose

	PORTION SIZE	KJ	CAL
meat + skin	100 g	1850	442
roasted, meat only	100 g	1330	318

	PORTION SIZE	KJ	CAL
partridge			
roasted... meat only	100 g	890	213
pheasant			
roasted... meat only	100 g	890	213
pigeon; squab			
roasted	100 g	960	229
quail			
roasted... meat only	100 g	728	174
turkey			
roasted	100 g	1145	274

deli meats

	PORTION SIZE	KJ	CAL
bacon			
fried... medium fat	34 g	530	127
grilled... medium fat	30 g	405	97
black pudding (sausage)			
av. all brands	100 g	1080	258
frankfurters			
PLUMROSE... cocktail	100 g	792	189
ham			
leg with fat... cured... boned... pressed	100 g	455	109
on the bone... cooked... sliced	100 g	950	227
prosciutto	100 g	1445	345
shoulder			
cured... boned... pressed slices	100 g	465	111
lean	100 g	495	118

	PORTION SIZE	KJ	CAL
steak			
grilled	100 g	680	163
raw	100 g	520	124
pressed meats			
beef, german; ham & chicken roll	100 g	970	232
berliner fleischwurst	100 g	945	226
cabanossi	100 g	1525	364
chicken roll	100 g	630	151
devon, chicken; devon, ham & chicken	100 g	980	234
garlic roll	100 g	1030	246
ham sausage	100 g	1140	272
liverwurst	100 g	1155	276
mortadella	100 g	1355	324
Polish	100 g	1005	240
salami... av. all varieties	100 g	1785	427
PLUMROSE... luncheon meat	100 g	995	237
sausages			
beef			
fried	100 g	1125	269
grilled	100 g	1292	370
kangaroo... **KANGA BANGAS**	100 g	454	109
liver	100 g	1115	266
pork			
fried	100 g	1317	315
grilled	100 g	1350	232
saveloys See frankfurters (in this section)			

	PORTION SIZE	KJ	CAL
canned, frozen & packaged meats			
See also **Takeaway Food; Frozen & Convenience Meals**			
beef burger patties			
fried...av. all brands	100 g	1205	288
grilled...av. all brands	100 g	1100	263
I & J			
bacon burgers	100 g	1189	283
big beefers	80 g	898	215
lean beefers	55 g	340	81
beef curry			
canned...av. all brands	100 g	765	183
braised beef steak			
canned...av. all brands	100 g	885	211
with onions...av. all brands	100 g	715	170
camp pie			
canned	100 g	710	170
chicken			
frozen			
BIRDS EYE			
chicken, cheese & broccoli patties	60 g	529	126
chicken & mixed vegie patties	60 g	488	116
INGHAMS			
breast medallions			
honey & sesame	100 g	877	209
teriyaki	100 g	899	214

	PORTION SIZE	KJ	CAL
breast tenders			
crumbed: honey & soy	100 g	822	196
schnitzels	100 g	1029	245
ham, leg			
canned...av. all brands	100 g	470	112
lean	25 g	105	25
lean + fat	35 g	165	39
YOU'LL LOVE COLES...honey leg ham...sliced	100 g	400	95
PLUMROSE			
deli	100 g	605	144
leg	100 g	575	137
ham, shoulder			
canned...av. all brands	100 g	495	118
savoury mince			
canned...av. all brands	100 g	755	180
steak & onion			
canned...av. all brands	100 g	740	177
steak & tomatoes			
canned...av. all brands	100 g	630	151
turkey			
INGHAMS...turkey roast...traditional	100 g	361	86
YOU'LL LOVE COLES...lean breast...sliced	100 g	212	51

Fish & other seafoods

Fish is a great low-calorie source of protein, and you can keep the calories down by keeping it out of the frying pan or deep fryer. A better choice is steaming, poaching, baking or grilling. As a general rule white fish has less calories than species with darker flesh, but all types of fish and seafood offer a variety of important nutrients. For example, oily fish such as mackerel and salmon have high levels of omega-3 fatty acids which are beneficial to brain function, while a single oyster contains your recommended daily allowance of zinc, a mineral that helps regulate blood sugar levels and metabolic rate, as well as boosting the immune system. Choose fish canned in springwater or brine in preference to oil. Unfortunately, a lot of our fish species are under great pressure from overfishing or are farmed in ways that are detrimental to both the environment and the animals, so choose carefully. I've marked with an asterisk the species to think twice about, but you should regularly check government guidelines for changes in the status of fish species.

	PORTION SIZE	KJ	CAL

fresh fish & shellfish

See also sushi in **Takeaway Food**

abalone

raw	100 g	410	98

anchovies

raw	100 g	925	221

*barramundi

raw	100 g	320	76
baked	100 g	410	98
battered, fried	100 g	835	200
poached; grilled...no fat	100 g	395	94
steamed	100 g	350	84

bream   See morwong

butterfish   See leatherjacket

calamari (squid)

raw	100 g	328	78
fried	100 g	1170	280
floured, fried	100 g	858	205

caviar

lumpfish roe

black	20 g	77	18
red	20 g	126	30

Chinese salted fish

steamed	100 g	660	158

*cod

	PORTION SIZE	KJ	CAL
raw	100 g	320	76
baked	100 g	710	170
dried, salted…cooked	100 g	585	140
fried in batter	100 g	835	200
grilled; poached; smoked	100 g	398	95
steamed	100 g	350	84
crab			
boiled	100 g	535	128
steamed…meat only	100 g	390	93
crayfish See lobster			
eel			
raw	100 g	700	167
fresh…grilled	100 g	840	201
*flake (shark)			
battered, deep-fried	100 g	828	198
crumbed, pan-fried	100 g	723	173
steamed	100 g	525	125
flathead			
battered, deep-fried	100 g	954	228
floured, pan-fried	100 g	740	177
steamed	100 g	485	116
flounder			
raw	100 g	330	79
baked	100 g	845	202
battered, fried	100 g	1165	278
crumbed, fried	100 g	950	227

	PORTION SIZE	KJ	CAL
grilled; poached	100 g	398	95
steamed	100 g	350	84
garfish			
raw	100 g	320	76
baked	100 g	410	98
grilled; poached	100 g	398	95
steamed	100 g	350	84
***gemfish**			
battered, deep-fried	100 g	1195	286
crumbed, pan-fried	100 g	1155	276
steamed	100 g	940	225
gurnard, long-finned			
raw	100 g	320	76
baked	100 g	410	98
grilled; poached	100 g	398	95
steamed	100 g	350	84
hake			
raw	100 g	350	84
halibut, tropical			
raw	100 g	320	76
baked	100 g	410	98
grilled; poached	100 g	398	95
steamed	100 g	350	84
jewfish (dhufish)			
battered, deep-fried	100 g	1000	239
crumbed, pan-fried	100 g	800	191

	PORTION SIZE	KJ	CAL
steamed	100 g	540	129
*John Dory			
fried	100 g	905	215
steamed	100 g	385	92
leatherjacket			
raw	100 g	310	74
fried	100 g	730	174
steamed	100 g	415	99
*ling			
raw	100 g	370	88
*lobster (crayfish)			
raw	100 g	370	88
boiled...meat only	100 g	407	97
thermidor...in shell	100 g	425	102
morwong (bream)			
battered, deep-fried	100 g	870	208
crumbed, pan-fried	100 g	10835	200
steamed	100 g	530	127
mullet			
battered, deep-fried	100 g	1225	293
floured, pan-fried	100 g	860	206
steamed	100 g	560	134
mulloway See jewfish (dhufish)			
mussels			
steamed	100 g	365	87
oysters			

	PORTION SIZE	KJ	CAL
fresh, shucked, av. 1 dozen	60 g	180	43
fried in batter	100 g	1000	239
*perch, northern pearl			
raw	100 g	320	76
baked	100 g	410	98
grilled; poached	100 g	398	95
steamed	100 g	350	84
*perch, sea (orange roughy)			
fried	100 g	905	216
steamed	100 g	385	92
pike			
raw	100 g	375	90
prawns			
raw	100 g	365	87
boiled			
with shell	100 g	170	41
without shell	100 g	450	108
crumbed, fried	100 g	1015	243
fried in batter	100 g	940	225
*red emperor			
raw	100 g	320	76
baked	100 g	410	98
grilled; poached	100 g	398	95
steamed	100 g	350	84
roe			
cod			

	PORTION SIZE	KJ	CAL
raw	100 g	475	114
fried	100 g	845	202
salmon, Atlantic			
raw	100 g	755	180
fried	100 g	845	202
salmon, Australian			
raw	100 g	905	216
baked	100 g	760	182
smoked	100 g	561	134
steamed	100 g	825	197
sardines			
raw	100 g	563	135
scallops			
raw	100 g	385	92
shrimps			
raw	100 g	400	96
boiled	100 g	365	87
with shell	100 g	165	39
without shell	100 g	365	87
crumbed, fried	100 g	1015	243
fried in batter	100 g	940	225
*snapper			
battered, deep-fried	100 g	855	204
crumbed, pan-fried	100 g	835	200
steamed	100 g	510	122

	PORTION SIZE	KJ	CAL
*snapper, red			
fried	100 g	905	216
steamed	100 g	385	92
squid See calamari			
tommy ruff (sea herring)			
raw	100 g	320	76
baked	100 g	410	98
grilled; poached	100 g	398	95
steamed	100 g	350	84
*trevally			
raw	100 g	475	114
fried	100 g	845	202
trout			
brown…steamed	100 g	565	135
inc. bones	100 g	375	90
rainbow…raw	100 g	815	195
*tuna			
raw	100 g	1010	241
whitebait			
fried	100 g	2175	520
whiting, King George			
battered, deep-fried	100 g	1315	314
floured, pan-fried	100 g	635	152
steamed	100 g	435	104

	PORTION SIZE	KJ	CAL

canned, frozen & packaged seafoods
See also **Frozen & Convenience Meals**

abalone

	PORTION SIZE	KJ	CAL
canned...drained	100 g	605	145

anchovies

canned

	PORTION SIZE	KJ	CAL
ALWAYS FRESH...in extra virgin olive oil	100 g	773	184
JOHN WEST...in olive oil	100 g	872	207

calamari

frozen

	PORTION SIZE	KJ	CAL
SEALORD...simply natural tender calamari			
with sauce sachet	100 g	366	87
I & J...crumbed calamari rings	100 g	1017	242

crab

canned

	PORTION SIZE	KJ	CAL
ALWAYS FRESH...crabmeat	100 g	252	60

eel

	PORTION SIZE	KJ	CAL
smoked	100 g	1380	330

fishcakes & patties

	PORTION SIZE	KJ	CAL
deep-fried	100 g	1158	277
frozen	100 g	990	237
ALDI...be light...frozen in sauce			
herb & garlic	180 g	625	149
lemon pepper	180 g	661	158
Thai coconut & curry	180 g	734	175

	PORTION SIZE	KJ	CAL
BIRDS EYE			
steamed...av. all flavours	180 g	605	144
I & J...frozen			
sea shantys	35 g	301	72
Thai fishcakes	100 g	800	190
fish fillets			
frozen			
BIRDS EYE...crumbed			
lemon pepper	100 g	647	156
original...with Omega 3	71 g	573	137
YOU'LL LOVE COLES...crumbed...lemon	100 g	936	224
I & J			
light & crispy			
av. all flavours	71 g	626	150
SEALORD			
tasty breadcrumbs	100 g	801	191
tempura batter hoki	100 g	949	227
fish fingers			
frozen			
BIRDS EYE	75 g	635	152
I & J...tasty	75 g	666	159
fish in sauce			
frozen			
in white sauce... av. all brands	100 g	605	145
I & J...with parsley sauce	200 g	749	179
SEALORD...hoki with parsley sauce	100 g	858	205

	PORTION SIZE	KJ	CAL
herrings			
canned	100 g	840	201
in tomato sauce	100 g	740	177
kippered	100 g	905	216
pickled	100 g	930	222
ALWAYS FRESH...fillets in mango pepper sauce	100 g	768	183
kedgeree			
homemade	100 g	635	151
kippers			
canned			
JOHN WEST...smoked fillets in brine	100 g	691	165
lobster			
canned	100 g	400	96
mackerel			
canned	100 g	760	182
JOHN WEST			
in brine	100 g	998	238
in oil	100 g	1040	249
mussels			
canned	100 g	840	201
ALWAYS FRESH...in oil	100 g	947	225
JOHN WEST...smoked...in oil	100 g	969	231
oysters			
canned, smoked	100 g	840	201
ALWAYS FRESH...in oil	100 g	989	235
JOHN WEST...in BBQ sauce	100 g	662	158

	PORTION SIZE	KJ	CAL
WOOLWORTHS HOME BRAND...in oil	100 g	1260	301
prawns			
dried	100 g	1515	362
ALWAYS FRESH...frozen...peeled	100 g	422	100
salmon, Atlantic			
frozen			
TASSAL			
crispy crumb	200 g	1636	392
smoke roasted	140 g	1175	280
salmon, pink			
canned			
ALLY	100 g	617	147
JOHN WEST...no added salt	100 g	570	136
PARAMOUNT	100 g	631	151
salmon, red			
canned			
JOHN WEST			
no added salt	100 g	743	177
skinless	100 g	728	174
sardines			
canned			
drained	100 g	915	219
in brine	100 g	820	196
in tomato sauce	100 g	740	177
JOHN WEST...sardine tempters			
olive oil blend	100 g	1078	257

	PORTION SIZE	KJ	CAL
onion tomato	100 g	620	148
tomato & basil	100 g	665	159
shrimps			
canned...drained	100 g	505	121
dried	100 g	1035	247
sushi See **Takeaway Food**			
tuna			
canned			
GREENSEAS			
in springwater...chunks	100 g	500	119
97% fat free...av. all types	100 g	450	107
JOHN WEST			
in brine	100 g	460	110
olive oil blend	100 g	887	212
slices...springwater	100 g	520	124
slices...sweet chilli	100 g	600	143
tempters, light...av. all flavours	100 g	382	91
SAFCOL			
gourmet			
spicy chilli	100 g	621	148
Thai red curry	100 g	542	129
SIRENA			
in oil	100 g	675	160
in oil, lite	100 g	529	126
in springwater	100 g	458	109
WEIGHT WATCHERS...in springwater	100 g	510	122

Eggs & egg dishes

Eggs are an excellent source of protein, with the white being almost all protein. The yolk has around 5 g of fat, which includes both saturated and unsaturated. A whole egg can be between 70 and 100 calories, depending on its size. I will often have an omelette using only one yolk and three whites, or even the whites alone. Eggs are also a useful addition to a healthy diet, particularly if you are looking to lose weight, as the high levels of protein they contain help you feel full for longer, making eggs a great choice for breakfast to prevent you snacking before lunch. For the same reason, adding a chopped hard-boiled egg to a lunchtime salad should keep you going until dinnertime. Beware scrambled egg dishes that are full of whole milk, cream and cheese, which will blow the calorie quota! Also, scrambling and frying your eggs ups the calorie count because of the oils and fats used to cook them. Stick with poached to keep the calories low.

	PORTION SIZE	KJ	CAL
Eggs & egg dishes			
dried eggs	100 g	2455	587
egg substitute			
ORGRAN...no egg	3 g	39	9
egg white			
raw; poached/boiled	31 g	60	14
egg yolk			
raw; poached/boiled	17 g	225	54
eggs, duck			
boiled	100 g	820	196
fried egg	1 medium	499	120
omelette			
chicken (Chinese)	100 g	895	214
plain	100 g	1040	249
prawn (Chinese)	100 g	765	183
poached egg	1 medium	305	73
quiche			
SARA LEE			
snack lorraine	119 g	1522	363
TEMPTATION			
petite cheese & spinach	17 g	214	51
petite quiche lorraine	17 g	263	628
pumpkin, leek & fetta	140 g	1373	328
scrambled egg	1 medium	374	90

Nuts & seeds

If you're a nut-lover, when you see the calorie count on nuts you'll go nuts! 'But nuts are healthy and contain protein and good fats,' I hear you cry. Yes, that's true, and dieticians recommend 8 to 10 nuts as a good healthy snack. But who the hell stops at 10? I know I can't once I get started. You'll need to be smarter with them. Scatter a few in a salad or toss some into a stir-fry, but avoid having a bag open on your desk or a bowl of them on the dining table. And I don't need to tell you that if you're eating nuts they should be the raw natural kind. Nuts that have been salted or coated in flavourings are gonna have a lot more calories. It's the same with seeds: lots of good things like fibre and minerals but combined with fats and calories. Add a scattering of pumpkin seeds when baking or pine nuts to a risotto for a healthy amount of crunchy goodness.

	PORTION SIZE	KJ	CAL

nuts & seeds
See also **Dips, Snacks, Savoury Spreads**

almonds

roasted, salted	100 g	2625	627
skinned	100 g	2505	599
sugared	100 g	1910	457
brazil nuts	100 g	2886	690
cashews...roasted	100 g	2399	574

chestnuts

roasted, peeled	100 g	724	173

coconut

fresh meat	100 g	1525	364
milk...canned	100 g	825	197
shredded...dry	100 g	843	201
AYAM			
coconut cream	100 ml	1216	291
coconut milk	100 ml	1024	245
light coconut cream	100 ml	711	170
light coconut milk	100 ml	541	131
hazelnuts...raw	100 g	2600	616
macadamias...raw	100 g	3000	712

nut butter See also savoury spreads in **Dips, Snacks, Savoury Spreads**

peanut	100 g	2650	365
ESKAL free nut	100 g	2620	625

	PORTION SIZE	KJ	CAL
peanuts			
choc-coated	100 g	2506	600
dry-roasted	100 g	2440	584
raw	100 g	2360	564
pecans...raw	100 g	2936	696
pine nuts...shelled	100 g	2820	668
pistachios...shelled	100 g	2368	564
pumpkin seeds...hulled	100 g	2200	520
sesame seeds	100 g	2640	630
sunflower seeds...hulled	100 g	2480	590
tahini (sesame seed paste)			
PUREHARVEST...organic...hulled; unhulled	100 g	2860	685
walnuts...shelled	100 g	2852	676

Milk, cheese, yoghurt

Dairy products are an excellent source of calcium and protein, but they are also a prime source of animal fats (the bad, saturated kind of fat) and calories. Read the labels carefully and don't fall into the trap of eating more of the low-fat ones because they are lower in calories. Dairy products should definitely be part of a healthy diet. The vitamins, minerals and other nutrients they provide are essential for your body to function and develop properly. Choosing a skim milk or low-fat natural yoghurt is better for you, as you still get all the nutrients with fewer calories, but remember that when it comes to dairy it's all about portion control to avoid taking in too much fat. It can be surprising just how different the calorie load is between different types of cheeses. Fetta, goat's cheese and cottage cheese have fewer calories than their harder cousins, for example.

For dairy desserts, see **Desserts & Puddings**.

	PORTION SIZE	KJ	CAL

milk

cow's milk

DAIRY FARMERS

cultured buttermilk	250 ml	523	125
lite	250 ml	530	128
skim	250 ml	370	88
whole	250 ml	683	163

DIPLOMA...powdered...reconstituted

skim	250 ml	378	90
whole	250 ml	707	169
FARMERS BEST...fresh and longlife	250 ml	573	138
FREEDOM FOODS...A2 milk light	250 ml	473	113

PAULS

cultured buttermilk	100 ml	197	47
froth top	100 ml	316	75
physiCAL...high calcium			
low-fat	250 ml	570	136
no-fat	250 ml	475	115
pure			
organic full cream	250 ml	720	171
organic low fat	250 ml	455	109
rev...low-fat	250 ml	478	114
slim	100 ml	264	63
smarter white...2% fat	250 ml	592	141
trim	100 ml	191	46

	PORTION SIZE	KJ	CAL
zymil…easy to digest	250 ml	473	113
PURA			
diet	250 ml	370	88
full-cream; kids	250 ml	662	158
heart active	250 ml	435	104
light start	250 ml	509	121
tone	250 ml	408	97
evaporated milk			
BEAR BRAND; CARNATION			
full-cream	100 ml	655	155
light	100 ml	400	95
flavoured milk see **Drinks**			
goat's milk			
NANNY GOAT LANE	250 ml	500	119
PAULS	100 ml	258	62
rice & oat milk			
FREEDOM FOODS…so natural rice milk			
light	250 ml	398	95
original	250 ml	598	143
PUREHARVEST			
Aussie dream rice milk…non-dairy	250 ml	525	125
oat milk…non-dairy	250 ml	447	107
VITASOY…rice milk	250 ml	525	125
soy milk			
PUREHARVEST			
enriched nature's organic	250 ml	550	131

	PORTION SIZE	KJ	CAL
SANITARIUM			
organics...simple soy	250 ml	525	126
so good...chilled			
fat-free	250 ml	375	90
lite	250 ml	425	102
regular	250 ml	675	161
UHT			
fat-free	250 ml	375	90
lite	250 ml	425	102
regular	250 ml	675	161
SOY LIFE			
original	250 ml	710	170
VITASOY			
calci plus	250 ml	672	160
lite	250 ml	398	95
regular	250 ml	550	132

cheese

bel paese	30 g	768	184
cheshire; colby	30 g	483	115
cotto	30 g	265	63
cream cheese; jarlsberg	30 g	433	103
gloucester; gruyère	30 g	519	124
gorgonzola	30 g	470	112
mascarpone	30 g	500	120
quark	30 g	170	41

	PORTION SIZE	KJ	CAL
low-fat	30 g	95	23
raclette; roquefort; provolone	30 g	463	111
stilton	30 g	575	137
AUSTRALIAN GOLD			
brie; camembert	25 g	318	76
edam	25 g	339	81
gouda	25 g	385	92
Swiss	25 g	380	90
tasty cheddar; vintage cheddar	25 g	420	100
BABYBEL...mini	20 g	262	62
BEGA			
cheddar			
extra light & tasty	21 g	242	58
fingers	20 g	284	68
light & tasty	21 g	294	70
super slices	21 g	292	70
super slim	20 g	172	41
stringers	20 g	246	59
tasty; vintage	25 g	425	102
BULLA			
low-fat cottage			
onion & chives	25 g	101	24
plain	25 g	95	23
COON			
cheddar			
light & tasty	25 g	350	84

	PORTION SIZE	KJ	CAL
tasty; extra tasty	25 g	422	101
CRACKER BARREL			
light	25 g	350	84
vintage cheddar	25 g	422	101
DEVONDALE			
tasty cheddar	25 g	429	103
FARMERS UNION			
cheddar...tasty matured; ol' bitey	30 g	508	121
YOU'LL LOVE COLES			
long-life...brie	25 g	382	91
long-life...camembert	25 g	316	75
lite cottage cheese	25 g	95	22
KRAFT			
dairy bites...fridge sticks	20 g	229	55
long life...brie; camembert	25 g	318	76
singles			
97% fat free	20 g	137	33
cheddar	21 g	293	70
extra tasty	20 g	296	71
light	21 g	218	52
light n' tasty	20 g	216	52
Swiss	20 g	278	66
Philadelphia			
cream; soft cream	25 g	289	69
extra light	25 g	183	44

	PORTION SIZE	KJ	CAL
LEMNOS			
fetta			
cow's milk	30 g	382	91
goat's milk	30 g	405	97
reduced fat	30 g	330	79
sheep's milk	30 g	378	90
smooth	30 g	276	66
haloumi	30 g	360	86
paneer	30 g	309	74
ricotta	30 g	226	54
MAINLAND			
cheddar			
epicure; tasty; vintage; extra tasty	25 g	440	105
light	25 g	338	98
colby	25 g	413	99
creamy havarti	25 g	425	101
edam; vegetarian edam	25 g	360	86
gouda	25 g	395	95
mozzarella	25 g	318	76
parmesan...shaved	5 g	79	19
Swiss	25 g	373	89
MARGARET RIVER			
baked ricotta	25 g	313	75
MERSEY VALLEY			
club vintage			
cracked peppercorn	25 g	415	99

	PORTION SIZE	KJ	CAL
original vintage	25 g	435	104
pickled onion	25 g	378	90
MIL LEL			
parmesan	25 g	382	91
pecorino; romano	25 g	386	92
NISI			
saganaki (Greek frying cheese)	30 g	484	115
NORCO			
Nimbin natural…reduced-salt	25 g	410	98
PANTALICA			
bacio	25 g	586	140
mascarpone	25 g	348	83
smooth ricotta	25 g	106	25
PERFECT ITALIANO			
mozzarella			
light…grated	25 g	258	62
pear	25 g	312	74
parmesan			
shredded; wedge	10 g	162	39
pizza plus	25 g	358	86
romano	10 g	160	38
ricotta			
light	25 g	58	14
smooth	25 g	124	29
SOUTH CAPE			
blue	25 g	392	94

	PORTION SIZE	KJ	CAL
bocconcini	25 g	265	63
brie	25 g	383	91
fetta (reduced fat)	20 g	245	58
goats	20 g	208	50
gouda	25 g	406	97
havarti	25 g	425	101
red Leicester	25 g	416	99
TASMANIAN HERITAGE			
deep blue	20 g	330	79
double brie	20 g	306	73
st claire	25 g	387	92
traditional camembert	20 g	319	76
WEIGHT WATCHERS			
reduced-fat cheddar slices	21 g	298	71
tasty cheddar...block	30 g	405	97

yoghurt

drinking yoghurts   See **Drinks**

frozen yoghurt   See **Ice-Cream & Ice Confections**

full-fat flavoured

ALDI			
just organic...av. all flavours	100 g	461	109
BULLA			
Greek-style gourmet			
mango & passionfruit	100 g	521	124
raspberry, blackberry & boysenberry	100 g	526	126

	PORTION SIZE	KJ	CAL
GIPPSLAND DAIRY			
twist…mango & passionfruit; berry; raspberry; passionfruit	100 g	673	161
JALNA			
biodynamic			
blueberry	100 g	471	112
bush honey	100 g	445	106
vanilla creamy; fruits of the forest	100 g	522	125
KING ISLAND DAIRY			
creamy indulgent	100 g	545	130
honey cinnamon	100 g	572	136
NESTLÉ			
children's			
best friends	95 g	429	103
bob the builder	95 g	432	103
hi 5…all flavours	95 g	430	103
SKI			
divine			
passionfruit; strawberry	100 g	467	112
vanilla creme	100 g	488	117
TAMAR VALLEY			
premium			
creamy honey	100 g	440	105
creamy vanilla	100 g	437	104
passionfruit mango	100 g	447	107

	PORTION SIZE	KJ	CAL
YOPLAIT			
original...av. all flavours	100 g	450	107
petit miam...strawberry peach	60 g	307	73
full-fat plain			
ATTIKI			
country style	100 g	445	106
CHRIS'S			
Greek style	100 g	613	146
FARMERS UNION			
European-style	100 g	309	74
Greek-style	100 g	561	134
JALNA			
genuine leben	100 g	350	84
premium...Greek-style	100 g	540	129
PAULS...natural set			
99.8% fat free	100 g	238	57
full fat	100 g	354	84
low-fat flavoured			
ANLENE...low-fat			
strawberry; vanilla	100 g	378	91
ATTIKI			
continental...apricot; strawberry	100 g	218	52
JALNA			
strawberry	100 g	394	94
NESTLÉ			
diet...av. all flavours	100 g	170	40

	PORTION SIZE	KJ	CAL
UNCLE TOBY'S...healthwise			
for bones...strawberry	100 g	396	94
for digestion...mixed berry	100 g	398	95
for heart...mango	100 g	400	95
VAALIA			
low-fat			
strawberry	100 g	413	98
vanilla blueberry	100 g	407	97
vanilla mango; berry splash	100 g	392	93

low-fat plain

	PORTION SIZE	KJ	CAL
ATTIKI			
continental...natural	100 g	170	40
GIPPSLAND			
fat-free organic	100 g	220	52
JALNA			
biodynamic	100 g	350	84
Greek style	100 g	394	94
NESTLÉ			
all natural	100 g	366	87
PAULS			
natural set	100 g	238	57
TAMAR VALLEY			
lite			
apricot	100 g	320	76
mixed berry	100 g	314	75

	PORTION SIZE	KJ	CAL
VAALIA			
low fat	100 g	334	80
YOPLAIT			
for me			
classic cheesecake	100 g	170	41
French vanilla	100 g	166	40
white peach	100 g	162	39
reduced-fat flavoured			
ALDI			
be light…av. all flavours	175 g	334	80
ATTIKI			
country style			
dark cherry; strawberry	100 g	375	89
honey	100 g	390	93
BULLA			
lite n' healthy			
apricot; wildberry	100 g	378	90
fruit salad	100 g	371	89
LOGICOL			
strawberry	100 g	375	90
vanilla	100 g	380	91
NESTLÉ			
all natural…av. all flavours	105 g	400	95
SKI			
d'lite			
berry basket	100 g	409	98

	PORTION SIZE	KJ	CAL
honey buzz	100 g	456	109
peach n' mango	100 g	385	92
TAMAR VALLEY			
Greek style			
mixed berry	100 g	575	137
passionfruit	100 g	564	135
raspberry	100 g	551	131
VAALIA			
apricot, mango, peach	100 g	380	91
French vanilla	100 g	425	101
luscious berries	100 g	403	96
YOPLAIT			
elivae			
pear & prune; vanilla	100 g	383	91
rhubarb & apple	100 g	360	86

reduced-fat plain

	PORTION SIZE	KJ	CAL
FARMERS UNION			
Greek-style lite	100 g	425	101
YOPLAIT			
yoplus	100 g	306	73

soy-based & lactose-free

	PORTION SIZE	KJ	CAL
SOY LIFE ... av. all flavours	100 g	335	80
VAALIA			
lactose-free			
French vanilla	100 g	396	88
strawberry	100 g	393	94

Fats & oils

All fats and oils are high in calories, so use them sparingly. However, not all fats are created equally and some are actually good for us. Saturated fats and trans fats are the worst offenders, raising cholesterol. These are the ones to look out for on food labelling. Unsaturated fats in olive oil and avocado oil actually help reduce cholesterol and help in the fight against heart disease. That doesn't mean you can use them willy-nilly, though. For all their benefits they are still high in calories, but making the best choice in the oils you use can be an important part of a healthy diet. Personally, I don't use many fats in my food preparation, so when I do I always go for one that tastes good, like French butter in preference to margarine, or a cold-pressed virgin olive oil rather than plain old canola. But I've said it before and I'll say it again: mind the quantities!

	PORTION SIZE	KJ	CAL

butter

standard	20 g	547	133
MAINLAND			
butter soft	20 g	610	145
WESTERN STAR...av. all varieties	20 g	612	146
YOU'LL LOVE COLES...reduced salt	20 g	608	145

ghee

av. all brands	100 g	3700	884

cream

aerosol	20 g	245	59
fresh	20 ml	305	73
reduced-fat	20 ml	220	53
single	20 ml	180	43
whipped	12 g	174	42
BULLA			
thickened cream	20 ml	158	38
thickened light cream	20 ml	156	37
thickened extra light cream	20 ml	114	28
thick cup cream	20 ml	278	66
GIPPSLAND DAIRY...pure double	30 ml	300	34
KING ISLAND DAIRY...pure	25 ml	535	60
PAULS			
dollop; double thick	20 ml	284	12
light thickened	20 ml	188	53

	PORTION SIZE	KJ	CAL
PURA			
double thick	20 ml	370	88
thick	20 ml	277	66
cream, sour			
BULLA			
extra light	50 ml	286	68
light	50 ml	392	94
JALNA...reduced	100 g	1037	248
PURA			
lite	20 ml	160	38
regular	20 ml	276	66
WEIGHT WATCHERS...extra light	20 g	111	27
crème fraîche			
av. all brands	100 g	1840	440
WATTLE VALLEY	50 g	725	173

margarines & dairy blends

	PORTION SIZE	KJ	CAL
ALDI			
be light...margarine	10 g	118	28
BERTOLLI			
classico...cholesterol-free	10 g	260	62
COLES			
sunspread canola	10 g	185	49
DEVONDALE			
dairy soft	10 g	302	72
extra soft	10 g	224	54

	PORTION SIZE	KJ	CAL
FLORA			
light	10 g	177	423
all other types	10 g	260	62
FLORA PRO-ACTIV			
light	10 g	150	36
regular	10 g	238	57
ultra light	10 g	90	21
GOLD'N CANOLA			
lite	10 g	200	48
standard	10 g	260	62
LOGICOL			
extra light	10 g	85	20
regular	10 g	175	42
MEADOW LEA			
canola; reduced salt	10 g	240	57
light	10 g	120	29
NUTTELEX			
light	10 g	220	52
regular	10 g	280	66
OLIVE GROVE			
extra-virgin	10 g	260	62
WEIGHT WATCHERS			
canola spread	10 g	170	40

oils

olive oil spray...av. all varieties	2 g	52	12

	PORTION SIZE	KJ	CAL
ALPHA ONE			
rice bran	15 ml	518	123
AZALEA			
grapeseed	15 ml	503	120
BERTOLLI			
olive	15 ml	666	158
CHANGS			
sesame	15 ml	510	123
COBRAM ESTATE			
olive	15 ml	565	135
CRISCO			
peanut; sunflower; canola	15 ml	510	122
RED ISLAND			
olive	15 ml	505	121
SUNCOAST			
macadamia	15 ml	503	120
THE GROVE			
avocado	15 ml	501	120
YOU'LL LOVE COLES			
extra-virgin olive	15 ml	555	150

animal fats

suet

fresh	20 g	700	167
mix...**TANDACO**	20 g	520	123

Herbs, spices, seasonings

Fresh herbs and spices are hard to beat for maximum flavour with minimum calories, so they feature regularly in my cooking. Don't be scared to experiment with them – in many dishes whatever you have to hand can easily replace what is listed in the recipe, and you might just make a great new taste discovery. Watch for additives (sugars, starches, etc.) in seasoning mixes and pastes that will bump up the calories. Beware of adding too much salt to dishes. While table salt doesn't have any calories, an excess of salt in your diet is one cause of fat storage, particularly around your middle. Spicy food has a double benefit. Not only does it give your dish a big hit of flavour, your body will actually burn calories cooling you down after a hot and spicy meal.

	PORTION SIZE	KJ	CAL
herbs and spices			
chillies			
banana (cooked)	55 g	35	8
green (cooked)	20 g	15	4
long, thin (cooked)	19 g	20	5
pickled	20 g	224	54
red (cooked/raw)	19 g	25	6
chives			
fresh, 1 tsp chopped	4 g	5	1
coriander			
fresh, 1 tsp chopped	4 g	5	1
garlic			
raw...peeled	6 g	25	6
ALWAYS FRESH...minced	5 g	27	6
MASTERFOODS...crushed	5 g	22	5
ginger			
ground	5 g	55	13
raw...peeled, grated	12 g	15	4
MASTERFOODS...grated	5 g	11	3
herbs & spices, dried			
av. all types, 1 tsp	5 g	65	16
horseradish			
raw	10 g	25	6
mint			
fresh, 1 tsp chopped	4 g	5	1

	PORTION SIZE	KJ	CAL
parsley			
common...raw	10 g	5	1
continental...raw	10 g	10	2

seasonings

anchovy essence
	PORTION SIZE	KJ	CAL
av brands	5 ml	15	4

bonox
KRAFT	8 g	34	8

pepper
black; white	2 g	25	6

salt, table
common; rock		0	0

seasoning mixes
KELLOGG'S...cornflake crumbs	50 g	791	189
OLD EL PASO...taco seasoning mix	50 g	565	135
TANDACO...coating mix			
fish; southern fried chicken	50 g	695	165
seasoned stuffing mix	50 g	735	176

stock
beef			
CAMPBELL'S...real stock	100 ml	56	13
CONTINENTAL...simply stock	1 cube	100	25
chicken			
CAMPBELL'S...real stock			
salt reduced; standard	100 ml	50	12

	PORTION SIZE	KJ	CAL
CONTINENTAL…simply stock	1 cube	25	6
fish			
CAMPBELL'S…real stock	100 ml	21	5
vegetable			
CAMPBELL'S…real stock	100 ml	50	12
sushi seasoning			
OBENTO	15 ml	70	16

pastes

curry paste

ASIA @ HOME			
green curry	14 g	108	26
laksa	21 g	139	33
massaman	14 g	114	27
pad Thai	21 g	236	56
red curry	14 g	93	22
PATAK'S			
balti	35 g	560	133
madras	35 g	750	180
tandoori	20 g	167	40
SHARWOOD'S			
tandoori	30 g	231	55
tikka	30 g	222	53
vindaloo	45 g	685	164
VALCOM			
green	25 g	103	24

	PORTION SIZE	KJ	CAL
laksa	25 g	84	20
pad Thai	25 g	265	63
red	25 g	190	45
miso (soybean paste)	15 g	105	25
sambal oelek			
CONIMEX	5 g	5	1
tomato paste			
ALDI...just organic	140 g	468	111
LEGGO'S			
garlic & herbs	25 g	57	14
no added salt	25 g	77	18

Sauces, dressings, pickles, chutneys

I love spicy food, so I'm always on the lookout for strong flavours with low calories. Mustard is a good choice and there are some great low-calorie salad dressings, but watch out for creamy sauces and mayonnaises as they are calorie heavyweights. Go easy with tomato-based sauces, too, as they are often high in sugar. Sauces and dressings in restaurants are among the worst offenders when it comes to calorie count. Make positive choices when eating out. Ask for no dressing or have it on the side (that way you can just dip your fork in, getting all the flavour without drowning your salad). Talk to your waiter about what a sauce contains, whether it is heavy on butter or cream, and ask for it to be left off your plate – it's your meal so have it the way you choose. At home I find that vinegar is a great low-calorie base for salad dressings. Try some white wine vinegar with a squeeze of lemon juice and a grind of black pepper for a zesty, healthy dressing.

	PORTION SIZE	KJ	CAL

sauces

apple sauce

SPC	100 g	311	74

cranberry

OCEANSPRAY	10 g	66	16

gravy

GRAVOX

liquid gravy...traditional	100 g	105	25
sachets			
lamb rosemary	62 ml	110	26
pepper	62 ml	114	27
supreme roast	62 ml	106	25

MAGGI...instant

roast chicken	62 ml	95	20
roast meat	62 ml	100	25

horseradish

MASTERFOODS...horseradish cream	5 g	38	9

ketjap manis See soy sauce (in this section)

mayonnaise

PRAISE

light	20 g	270	64
whole egg	20 g	620	148

meat/poultry/fish sauces

parsley...homemade	20 ml	155	37

	PORTION SIZE	KJ	CAL
CONTINENTAL			
apricot chicken curry	100 g	982	234
creamy mushroom chicken	100 g	573	136
creamy tuna mornay	100 g	831	396
GRAVOX...liquid sauce			
diane	55 g	84	20
mushroom garlic	55 g	121	29
pepper steak	55 g	110	27
LEGGO'S...simmer sauce			
chicken cacciatore	100 g	223	53
chicken parmigiana	100 g	267	64
Mediterranean spicy tomato & herbs	100 g	276	66
MASTERFOODS			
seafood cocktail	20 g	176	42
sweet & sour	20 g	119	28
OLD EL PASO...taco sauce	100 g	128	30
PATAK'S...simmer sauce			
korma	135 g	886	212
rogan josh	111 g	351	84
spicy butter chicken	135 g	651	155
YACKANDANDAH...simmer sauce			
honey soy	100 g	760	181
Thai satay	100 g	650	155
mint sauce			
CORNWELL'S	20 ml	60	14
MASTERFOODS...mint jelly	20 g	225	54

	PORTION SIZE	KJ	CAL
mustard			
powder...av. all brands	5 g	97	23
MASTERFOODS			
Australian; Dijon	5 g	24	6
honey wholegrain	5 g	43	10
hot English	5 g	34	8
pasta sauces			
BARILLA			
arrabiata	10 g	20	5
basilico	10 g	23	5
napoletana	10 g	27	6
olive	10 g	35	8
BERTOLLI FIVE BROTHERS			
portobello mushrooms & garlic	125 g	281	67
summer tomato basil	125 g	263	63
CAMPBELL'S...spaghetti...av. all varieties	100 g	270	71
DOLMIO			
chunky			
rustic farmhouse vegetable	100 g	231	55
tomato, onion & roast garlic	100 g	244	58
vine ripened tomato	100 g	220	52
pasta bake			
bechamel lasagne	100 g	681	163
three cheese	100 g	478	114
tomato with extra cheese	100 g	438	105
tuna bake sauce	100 g	393	94

	PORTION SIZE	KJ	CAL
traditional recipe			
classic tomato	100 g	376	90
extra garlic	100 g	249	59
mushroom	100 g	333	79
spicy peppers	100 g	246	59
LEGGO'S			
pasta sauce			
bolognese	100 g	334	80
primavera	100 g	285	68
pesto			
creamy basil & pinenut	100 g	1240	296
sundried tomato	100 g	892	213
stir-through...pasta sauce			
chargrilled vegetables	100 g	498	119
tomato, olive & chilli	100 g	591	143
PAUL NEWMAN'S...pasta sauce			
classic tomato	100 g	210	50
garlic & basil	100 g	210	50
RAGULETTO...pasta sauce			
bolognese	100 g	172	41
red wine with garlic	100 g	222	53
plum sauce			
SPC	125 g	1313	314
stir-fry sauces			
ASIA @ HOME			
black bean	75 g	285	68

	PORTION SIZE	KJ	CAL
Thai satay	75 g	642	153
AYAM			
black bean	20 ml	92	23
hoisin	20 ml	184	44
KAN TONG			
black bean	100 g	419	100
lite sweet & sour	100 g	301	72
peanut satay	100 g	584	140
Thai coconut curry	100 g	383	92
MASTERFOODS...marinade			
honey mustard & herb	100 g	602	144
smokey bbq	100 g	576	138
teriyaki	100 g	708	169

soy sauce

	PORTION SIZE	KJ	CAL
ABUNDANT EARTH...tamari	20 ml	58	14
CONIMEX...ketjap manis	20 ml	173	40
CORNWELL'S	20 ml	56	14
HAKUBAKU...chilli soy	20 ml	250	48
KIKKOMAN...organic	20 ml	62	14

tartare sauce...MASTERFOODS

	PORTION SIZE	KJ	CAL
	20 g	516	124

tomato purée

	PORTION SIZE	KJ	CAL
LEGGO'S	100 g	116	28

tomato sauce

	PORTION SIZE	KJ	CAL
ROSELLA			
low-joule	30 ml	48	11
standard	30 ml	177	42

	PORTION SIZE	KJ	CAL
wasabi sauce			
HAKUBAKU	20 ml	268	64
S & B	20 ml	212	51
worcestershire...CORNWELL'S	20 ml	78	19

dressings

	PORTION SIZE	KJ	CAL
caesar			
KRAFT...original squeezable	20 ml	249	59
PAUL NEWMAN'S	20 ml	420	100
PRAISE...squeezable	20 ml	270	64
coleslaw			
KRAFT...classic	20 ml	285	68
PRAISE...99% fat-free	20 ml	100	24
French (vinaigrette)			
KRAFT...100% fat-free	20 ml	34	8
PAUL NEWMAN'S			
balsamic	20 ml	290	69
light	20 ml	130	31
PRAISE			
fat-free	20 ml	60	14
standard	20 ml	190	45
Italian			
PRAISE			
deli-style...lemon, garlic & herb	20 ml	93	22
fat-free	20 ml	40	9
standard	20 ml	170	41

	PORTION SIZE	KJ	CAL
thousand island			
KRAFT	20 ml	240	57
PRAISE			
standard	20 ml	272	65
99% fat-free	20 ml	78	19
vinegar			
CORNWELL'S			
apple cider	20 ml	13	3
balsamic	20 ml	60	14
red wine	20 ml	14	3
MELROSE...organic apple cider vinegar	20 ml	19	4

pickles, relish, chutneys

	PORTION SIZE	KJ	CAL
LEGGO'S...mustard pickle...all varieties	20 g	82	19
MAHARAJAH'S CHOICE			
mango pickle; mixed pickle	20 g	67	16
tamarind chutney	20 g	294	70
MASTERFOODS			
corn relish	20 g	80	19
gherkin relish	20 g	123	29
tomato relish...gourmet	20 g	86	21
ROSELLA			
low-joule	20 g	23	6
mustard pickle...sweet	20 g	61	15
PATAK'S...sweet mango chutney	20 g	203	48

Dips, snacks, savoury spreads

Dips, crackers and a glass of wine are the entertainer's go-to choice, but those calories can sneak up on you if you're not careful. A modest scoop of dip (around 10 g) on a spicy cracker (around 2 g) adds up to around 30 calories. Add that to a glass of sauvignon blanc (100 calories) and it's not hard to get into calorie overload, especially when you haven't even sat down to dinner yet. Another thing to remember is that when we have a couple of glasses of wine or a cocktail or two, our food choices tend to fall by the wayside. The dehydrating effect of alcohol means we often crave salty snacks that are high in calories. Alternate glasses of water with your alcoholic drinks to keep your head right (and avoid too many of the empty calories alcohol contains). If you have the time, try making your own party snacks next time you are hosting. Pita bread crisps are much healthier than tortilla chips, while dips can easily be whizzed up from fresh vegetables and a dash of olive oil. It is much easier to control the calorie count and salt levels in homemade snacks than the store-bought kind.

	PORTION SIZE	KJ	CAL

dips

	PORTION SIZE	KJ	CAL
baba ghannouj (eggplant dip)	20 g	200	48
hommus	20 g	205	49
skordalia	20 g	110	26
taramosalata	20 g	250	60
CHRIS'			
lite & fresh			
hommus	20 g	146	35
tzatziki	20 g	60	14
traditional homestyle			
avocado	20 g	240	57
caviar	20 g	258	62
eggplant	20 g	123	29
kalamata olive	20 g	196	47
lentils Morocco	20 g	170	41
COPPERPOT			
chunky			
basil with cashews & parmesan	20 g	424	101
red pepper with cashews & parmesan	20 g	322	77
spinach & fetta with cashews	20 g	294	59
classic			
avocado	20 g	202	48
cheese & chives	20 g	188	45
hommus	20 g	218	52
layered			

	PORTION SIZE	KJ	CAL
chilli, crab & spring onion	20 g	113	27
peppers & pesto	20 g	212	51
KRAFT			
French onion	20 g	182	43
Moroccan spice	20 g	189	45
onion & bacon	20 g	191	46
tomato, olive & fetta	20 g	195	47
PHILADELPHIA...pourovers...av. all flavours	30 g	216	51
UNCLE TOBY'S			
le snak			
cheddar cheese; French onion	22 g	370	88
mild salsa	20 g	130	31
YUMI'S			
creamed spinach	20 g	337	80
Italian olive dip	20 g	351	84
spicy pumpkin dip	20 g	142	34
sweet potato & cashew	20 g	194	46

salsa

	PORTION SIZE	KJ	CAL
MASTERFOODS			
medium chunky	30 g	39	9
mild	30 g	38	9
OLD EL PASO			
bbq bacon...mild	30 g	49	12
chunky tomato...hot; medium	30 g	40	9
roasted capsicum...mild	30 g	93	22

	PORTION SIZE	KJ	CAL

snack foods

See also **Biscuits; Nuts & Seeds**

corn chips

DORITOS…cheese supreme	50 g	587	140
FREEDOM FOODS			
baked	50 g	855	204
natural	50 g	1030	246
THOMAS CHIPMAN			
cheese; original	46 g	1003	240

nuts

NOBBY'S			
mixed nuts…salted	100 g	2480	592
peanuts…salted	100 g	2450	585

pappadams

MAHARAJAH'S CHOICE			
Madras spiced; plain; garlic	10 g	118	28
PATAK'S			
plain	10 g	120	29
plain ready-to-eat	25 g	490	117

popcorn

UNCLE TOBY'S			
butter	100 g	2030	485
natural	100 g	2040	487

potato chips

potato straws

	PORTION SIZE	KJ	CAL
flavoured	25 g	730	174
plain	25 g	755	180
DELI-STYLE			
honey soy chicken	50 g	1024	245
sea salt	50 g	1022	244
sweet chilli	50 g	1025	245
FREEDOM FOODS...no salt	25 g	569	136
SMITH'S...original crinkle-cut crisps	27 g	575	137
THOMAS CHIPMAN			
av. all flavours	50 g	1090	260
WEIGHT WATCHERS...potato bakes			
salt & vinegar	20 g	341	81
sour cream & chives	20 g	332	79

pretzels

PARKERS...lightly baked mini pretzels	50 g	830	198

rice crackers

DELI-STYLE...rice crisps			
sour cream chives	50 g	553	132
SAKATA			
snakatas...av. all flavours	100 g	1737	415

vege chips

AJITAS			
BBQ	25 g	463	110
natural	25 g	488	116
sweet & sour	25 g	473	113

	PORTION SIZE	KJ	CAL

savoury spreads

	PORTION SIZE	KJ	CAL
anchovy paste	5 g	40	10
cream cheese spread...**FARMLAND**	20 g	264	63
lobster paste...av. all brands	20 g	151	36
nut spreads...av. all brands	5 g	125	30
pâté de foie...av. all brands	20 g	248	59
peanut butter...av. all brands	20 g	530	127
KRAFT...vegemite	5 g	40	9
MASTERFOODS...promite	5 g	39	9
MELROSE...nut spreads			
almond	10 g	240	57
cashew; hazelnut	10 g	260	62
PECKS			
anchovette paste	5 g	30	7
devilled ham paste	5 g	38	9
SANITARIUM...marmite	5 g	34	8
ALWAYS FRESH...tapenade			
basil & parmesan	5 g	108	26
black olive	5 g	41	9
tomato	5 g	54	13

Soups

My soups are always homemade using fresh ingredients and lots of herbs and spices. That way I know exactly what goes into them, and I can control things like salt and sugar content. Tinned soup may contain high levels of salt, sugar and preservatives, so always read the label carefully. Soup is also perfect for making in batches and freezing in handy portion sizes for future meals that are quick and convenient. It will also save you money. Adding some extra vegetables can make for a more filling soup, ideal for the winter months, while the high water content means that soups fill you up quickly. Start a meal with a bowl of soup and you are less likely to overeat when it comes to the main course.

	PORTION SIZE	KJ	CAL

Asian

	PORTION SIZE	KJ	CAL
chicken galangal (Thai)	100 g	470	112
chicken sour (Vietnamese)	100 g	187	45
chicken vermicelli (Vietnamese)	100 g	205	49
miso soup	100 ml	62	15
prawn (Thai)	100 g	170	41

condensed

CAMPBELL'S

	PORTION SIZE	KJ	CAL
creamy…diluted with ½ whole milk ½ water			
cream of chicken	100 g	220	52
cream of chicken and mushroom	100 g	185	44
regular…diluted with equal quantity of water			
chicken noodle	100 g	114	27
split pea & ham	100 g	261	62

HEINZ

	PORTION SIZE	KJ	CAL
creamy condensed…diluted with ½ whole milk ½ water			
cream of chicken	100 g	240	57
cream of pumpkin	100 g	195	47
regular…diluted with equal quantity of water			
vegetable	100 g	100	23

instant/packet

BASCO (gluten-free)

	PORTION SIZE	KJ	CAL
creamy tomato	250 ml	373	90

	PORTION SIZE	KJ	CAL
French onion	250 ml	303	73
pumpkin	250 ml	168	40
CONTINENTAL			
Asian			
laksa	250 ml	666	159
Thai red curry	250 ml	678	162
cup-a-soup (sachets)			
chicken noodle	250 ml	210	50
pea & ham	250 ml	321	77
tomato	250 ml	340	81
hearty			
Italian minestrone	250 ml	676	161
vegetable & beef	250 ml	574	137
lots-a-noodles			
beef	250 ml	497	119
mild chicken curry	250 ml	536	128
one-litre simmer soup			
Dutch curry rice	250 ml	290	69
French onion	250 ml	136	33
spring vegetable	250 ml	115	28
thick vegetable	250 ml	229	55
vegiful			
Mediterranean tomato	280 ml	526	126
potato & leek	280 ml	418	100
winter vegetable	280 ml	488	117

	PORTION SIZE	KJ	CAL
xtra full			
beef stroganoff	300 ml	662	158
chicken n' sweetcorn chowder	300 ml	656	157
roast lamb & veg	300 ml	586	140
COUNTRY CUP			
feel good			
broccoli; tomato	200 ml	300	75
potato & leek	200 ml	285	70
flavours of the world			
chicken & corn	200 ml	660	160
Thai satay with rice	200 ml	525	125
tom yum	200 ml	325	80
croutons			
cream of chicken & corn	200 ml	425	100
creamy butternut pumpkin & ham	200 ml	460	110
noodles			
beef	200 ml	430	100
chicken & corn	200 ml	450	110
S & B			
instant wakame soup	206 ml	61	14
tofu & miso soup	170 ml	153	36

ready-to-serve

CAMPBELL'S			
chunky			
beef	100 g	225	54

	PORTION SIZE	KJ	CAL
ham & pea	100 g	275	66
hearty Irish stew	100 g	239	59
roast chicken & veg	100 g	221	53
country ladle			
creamy chicken	100 g	200	48
farmhouse vegetable	100 g	142	34
golden pumpkin & tortellini	100 g	200	48
minestrone	100 g	160	38
velish			
butternut pumpkin	100 g	180	43
Moroccan vegetable	100 g	161	39
provincial vegetable	100 g	177	42
HEINZ			
big n' chunky (microwave bowl)			
beef burgundy	100 g	180	43
beef stockpot	100 g	210	50
butter chicken curry	100 g	305	73
chicken & corn	100 g	245	59
exotics			
Chinese chicken with sweetcorn	100 g	250	60
Malaysian Penang curry	100 g	240	57
Thai massaman beef curry	100 g	280	67
very special			
creamy pumpkin	100 g	270	64
pea & ham	100 g	225	54
Tuscan tomato & bacon	100 g	255	61

	PORTION SIZE	KJ	CAL
LA ZUPPA…microwave bowl			
cauliflower & pea	420 g	563	134
lentil	420 g	740	176
minestrone	420 g	701	146
pumpkin	420 g	546	130
Tuscan bean	420 g	861	206
WEIGHT WATCHERS			
minestrone	210 g	285	68
pumpkin soup	220 g	285	68
tomato	220 g	239	55

Frozen & convenience meals

A lot of convenience meals have similar calorie counts to homemade food, so they can be quite handy for busy people. But the nutritional value of packaged food is never going to match fresh wholefoods and in my opinion it doesn't taste half as good. If you are struggling with your weight, pies, pasties and microwave pizzas with their stratospheric energy counts are definitely not your friends. Processed convenience meals are also likely to contain a high level of salt. While we need a certain amount of salt in our diet to aid bodily processes, too much can lead to kidney, liver and heart problems. If you are about to embark on a change of diet, I recommend that you go through your freezer first and chuck away all the unhealthy ready-made meals and convenience foods it contains. That way they are not there as a quick-fix solution.

	PORTION SIZE	KJ	CAL

frozen & convenience meals

See also **Meat, Poultry, Deli Meats; Eggs & Egg Dishes**

	PORTION SIZE	KJ	CAL
ALDI			
be light			
creamy mushroom tortellini	370 g	1240	296
sundried tomato & chicken penne	350 g	1620	387
tomato & vegetable cannelloni	400 g	1520	363
ASIA @ HOME			
meal kits			
laksa	290 g	1820	435
san choy bow	188 g	940	224
BIRDS EYE...vegetables in cheese sauce	100 g	514	123
CHIKO roll	163 g	1253	299
CONTINENTAL			
cous cous			
Mediterranean vegetables & herbs	95 g	601	144
Moroccan spices	95 g	596	142
pasta & sauce			
alfredo	95 g	523	125
carbonara	95 g	489	117
sour cream & chives	95 g	444	106
rices of the world			
Indian mild curry	95 g	554	132
Thai coconut & lime	95 g	535	128

	PORTION SIZE	KJ	CAL
FANTASTIC NOODLES			
meal cups			
chicken	380 g	1385	331
chicken & corn	380 g	1365	327
GRIFF'S			
curried prawns	400 g	1461	349
fried rice	350 g	2011	481
sweet-and-sour pork	400 g	2038	487
HARVEST			
beef goulash with vegetables	212 g	568	136
Irish stew	212 g	604	144
lamb hot pot	212 g	551	132
mild curry	212 g	630	150
vegetables & sausages	212 g	657	157
HEINZ			
big eat (bowls)			
ravioli bolognese	100 g	320	76
spaghetti bolognese	100 g	240	57
spaghetti			
alphagetti	100 g	235	56
bolognaise	100 g	270	64
KRAFT			
macaroni cheese			
deluxe cheese dinner	100 g	661	158
deluxe cheese dinner with tuna in springwater	100 g	597	142

	PORTION SIZE	KJ	CAL
LEGGO'S			
light & tasty pasta meals			
chicken, sundried tomato with casarecce pasta	240 g	1253	299
tuna, tomato & herb with orrecchiete pasta	240 g	1234	294
pasta meals			
carbonara	390 g	2325	555
matriciana	390 g	1963	469
Napoletana	390 g	2035	486
primavera	390 g	1981	473
McCAIN			
gourmet creations			
creamy penne pasta	100 g	513	123
healthy choice			
bowl			
chicken stir-fry with hokkein noodles	340 g	1278	306
creamy chicken carbonara	340 g	1638	392
oyster beef	300 g	1208	289
plated			
beef medallions	310 g	1043	248
fillet of lamb	310 g	994	238
twin pack			
chicken bolognese	200 g	913	218
creamy carbonara	200 g	841	201
meatballs & pasta	200 g	913	218

	PORTION SIZE	KJ	CAL
red box			
beef & cashews	350 g	1748	418
fettucine carbonara	375 g	2396	574
lasagne	400 g	2742	656
shepherd's pie	400 g	1956	468
MAGGI			
noodles			
2-minute			
beef	320 g	1640	392
chicken	320 g	1280	306
lean cuisine (bowls)			
chicken & vegetable risotto	300 g	1210	289
beef stroganoff with pasta	280 g	1110	266
Moroccan lamb with couscous	280 g	1370	328
roast pumpkin & fetta with pasta	300 g	1340	321
Thai green chicken curry with rice	280 g	1140	273
OLD EL PASO			
meal kits			
beef tacos	111 g	1110	265
chicken burritos	191 g	1290	308
chicken enchilada	192 g	1273	304
SAN REMO			
la pasta single snack			
alfredo	260 g	1440	344
chicken curry	260 g	1280	306
creamy bacon; carbonara	260 g	1480	353

	PORTION SIZE	KJ	CAL
SPC			
spaghetti...tomato & cheese	100 g	322	77
ST DALFOUR			
couscous	175 g	1292	306
ham with potatoes	175 g	824	197
three bean with sweetcorn	175 g	639	152
tuna & pasta	175 g	710	170
wild salmon with vegetables	175 g	705	168
SUIMIN			
meal cups			
braised beef	380 g	1397	334
chicken	380 g	1430	342
SUNRICE			
microwave rice			
Mediterranean tomato rice	125 g	1060	254
oriental style egg fried rice	125 g	993	238
TASTY BITE...gluten-free			
Bombay potatoes	142 g	420	100
Kashmir spinach	142 g	546	130
Jaipur vegetables	142 g	714	170
Madras lentils	142 g	504	120
YOU'LL LOVE COLES			
lite beef hot pot	100 g	304	73
lite beef lasagne	100 g	424	101
lite chicken risotto	100 g	357	85

	PORTION SIZE	KJ	CAL
pies, pasties, sausage rolls			
pies			
fish	100 g	540	129
pork	180 g	2815	673
spinach (Lebanese)	100 g	1215	290
FOUR'N TWENTY			
beef & cheese	175 g	1730	413
chicken veg	175 g	1764	421
lite	175 g	1590	380
party	50 g	548	131
traditional	175 g	1800	430
HERBERT ADAMS			
gourmet			
beef & red wine	210 g	2026	484
pepper steak...chunky	210 g	2120	507
SARGENTS			
all chicken	225 g	2210	528
grain fed beef	225 g	2120	507
pasties			
HERBERT ADAMS			
traditional	175 g	1610	385
vegetable	175 g	1450	346
sausage rolls			
FOUR'N TWENTY			
jumbo	117 g	1300	311

	PORTION SIZE	KJ	CAL
party	43 g	503	120
HERBERT ADAMS			
party	38 g	409	98

savoury rolls

HERBERT ADAMS

cheese & spinach	220 g	2330	557

pizzas

McCAIN

Hawaiian…microwave	270 g	2669	638
meatlovers…slices	100 g	1026	245

PAPA GIUSEPPI'S

BBQ meat feast	125 g	1300	311
tropical supremo	127 g	1180	282

WOOLWORTHS HOME BRAND

supreme	62 g	625	149

Takeaway food

Eating out is always nice, but it can be tricky to source a nutritious low-calorie meal. It all comes down to making smarter choices and not being lulled into eating something you'll regret when you go to put your jeans on. Take control of your order by asking for no margarine, no dressing, grilled instead of fried, salad instead of chips, stir-fries instead of curries. It is possible to eat out and remain healthy, but you need to choose wisely. Bear in mind that some cuisines tend to use more high-calorie ingredients than others. Italian dishes tend to use cream and cheese, for example, while Japanese meals are often lower-calorie, with the emphasis on fresh wholefoods. There are some takeaway foods that I just never eat, ever, and you probably know what they are. If you really want to lose weight you'll have to do the same. Even better, plan your meals and shop accordingly so that you will always have on hand the ingredients to make a healthy, nutritious meal. That way you can't use the excuse that 'there's nothing in the fridge' to justify picking up a takeaway on the journey home.

	PORTION SIZE	KJ	CAL

hot food

	PORTION SIZE	KJ	CAL
beef hot salad (Thai)	100 g	390	93
beef satay	100 g	805	192
california roll (Japanese)	100 g	658	156
chicken curry (Thai)	100 g	570	136
chicken salad (Thai)	100 g	495	118
chiko roll...deep fried	100 g	945	226
dim sim...deep fried	100 g	930	222
fishcakes (Thai)	100 g	695	166
fried rice (Chinese)	100 g	930	222
garlic prawns (Chinese)	100 g	510	122
ladyfingers (Lebanese)	100 g	1195	285
lemon chicken (Chinese)	100 g	820	196
nachos...with cheese	100 g	1280	306
pork buns	100 g	1116	267
pork spare ribs in black-bean sauce (Chinese)	100 g	835	200
samosas (stuffed with minced lamb)	100 g	2390	571
scotch eggs	100 g	1160	277
spring roll (Thai)	100 g	1130	270
sweet-and-sour pork (Chinese)	100 g	770	184
taco	100 g	905	216

breakfast meals

McDONALD'S

	PORTION SIZE	KJ	CAL
English muffin	57 g	685	140

	PORTION SIZE	KJ	CAL
English muffin with jam	60 g	820	196
hotcakes			
with butter & syrup	223 g	2552	610
sausage & egg mcmuffin	164 g	1882	450

burgers & hot dogs

	PORTION SIZE	KJ	CAL
hot dog...roll + frankfurter, av. all brands	75 g	875	209
HUNGRY JACK'S			
Aussie	311 g	2690	643
bacon deluxe	233 g	2930	700
grilled chicken	153 g	1390	332
whopper	269 g	2740	654
KFC			
original	187 g	1876	448
zinger	207 g	2248	537
McDONALD'S			
big mac	214 g	2008	480
cheeseburger	114 g	1255	300
filet-o-fish	143 g	1589	380
hamburger	100 g	1046	250

chicken & chips

chicken

	PORTION SIZE	KJ	CAL
HUNGRY JACK'S...nuggets, 6 pieces	108 g	974	232

	PORTION SIZE	KJ	CAL
KFC			
Kentucky BBQ...quarter	155 g	1339	320
nuggets, 6 pieces	100 g	1090	260
original recipe chicken	159 g	1886	451
popcorn chicken, reg.	152 g	1824	435
McDONALD'S...chicken mcnuggets, 6 pieces	96 g	1046	250

potato chips

HUNGRY JACK'S...french fries, reg.	116 g	1565	374
KFC...seasoned	131 g	1296	310
McDONALD'S...french fries, med.	116 g	1540	368

desserts & drinks

desserts

HUNGRY JACK'S			
soft-serve ice-cream...cone	117 g	808	193
sundae...caramel; chocolate	141 g	1121	269
KFC			
cheesecake...cookies and cream	80 g	1090	260
mousse...choc caramel	80 g	1220	291
McDONALD'S			
mcflurries			
M&M's	348 g	2594	620
oreo cookie	337 g	2343	560
sundae...hot fudge	179 g	1380	330

	PORTION SIZE	KJ	CAL
milkshakes			
HUNGRY JACK'S			
chocolate; vanilla, reg.	305 ml	1776	425
McDONALD'S			
chocolate, reg.	333 g	1840	440

fish & chips

fish...battered deep fried	150 g	1600	380
fish...grilled (white)	150 g	530	126
fishcake	90 g	1050	250
french fries; chips	100 g	800	190

kebabs, souvlaki & other Greek dishes

dolmades (cabbage rolls)	150 g	700	168
felafel	100 g	990	273
kebab	100 g	790	189
souvlaki	100 g	830	198
spanakopita (spinach pie)	150 g	1100	260

pies & pasties

pastie (meat)	175 g	1850	440
pastie (vegetable)	175 g	1680	400
sausage roll (large)	125 g	1470	350
chicken pie; steak pie	175 g	1850	440
quiche	150 g	1600	380

	PORTION SIZE	KJ	CAL
pizza (av. 1 slice)			
PIZZA HUT			
pan pizza			
cheese lovers	85 g	1017	243
super supreme	94 g	949	227
veggie supreme	88 g	850	203
thin 'n crispy			
cheese lovers	59 g	1017	243
super supreme	71 g	721	172
veggie supreme	63 g	581	139

rolls & sandwiches

(2 slices bread, 2 tsp butter; all salad inc. 1 tsp mayonnaise)			
asparagus roll	1 av.	185	44
cheese			
grated tasty	1 av.	1230	294
processed slice	1 av.	1170	280
cheese & salad			
grated tasty	1 av.	1430	342
processed slice	1 av.	1370	327
chicken & salad	1 av.	1350	323
egg & lettuce	1 av.	1295	310
ham (1 slice)	1 av.	1110	265
ham & salad	1 av.	1310	313
ham, salad & cheese	1 av.	1580	378

	PORTION SIZE	KJ	CAL
roast beef; pork (1 slice)	1 av.	1160	277
salad only; salad roll	1 av.	1100	263
steak	1 av.	940	225
tomato	1 av.	940	225
tuna & salad	1 av.	1240	296
vegemite	1 av.	900	215

salads & vegetables

KFC

coleslaw, reg.	110 g	460	110
potato & gravy, reg.	110 g	329	79

McDONALD'S

hash brown	100 g	1030	246
salads			
crispy chicken caesar	313 g	1255	300
garden	87 g	83	20

sauces

McDONALD'S

barbecue; sweet-and-sour	28 g	209	50
sweet Thai chilli	28 g	212	51

sushi

GO SUSHI

california roll	100 g	658	156
tuna roll	100 g	761	181

Biscuits

Biscuits are a) almost always high in calories and b) impossible to say no to after you've had just one. Now if that's not a recipe for weight gain then I don't know what is. The refined flour and sugar in biscuits promotes fat storage in your body. Biscuits are also habit-forming. How many of us automatically reach for the biscuit tin while the kettle is boiling for a cup of tea? How often are biscuits the default option at a business meeting or mid-morning get-together? They can seem small and innocuous, but they soon add up. Keeping a food diary can help you pinpoint where such habitual eating typically happens in your diet, so you can formulate plans to unlearn the habit. Plain, unsweetened biscuits, such as crackers and crispbreads, usually have the lowest calories, and sweet, iced and chocolate-coated ones the highest.

	PORTION SIZE	KJ	CAL

crackers & crispbreads

crackers			
high-fat...av. all brands	100 g	2060	492
low-fat...av. all brands	100 g	1675	400
crispbreads			
puffed & toasted; extra fibre...av. all brands	5 g	80	19
rye...av. all brands	100 g	1505	360
wheat...av. all brands	100 g	1735	415
rusks			
Dutch	100 g	1620	387
plain; wholemeal	100 g	1725	412
wholewheat...av. all brands	5 g	90	22
ARNOTTS			
cruskits...original	12 g	230	55
salada...light	15 g	570	136
sao	25 g	490	117
vita-weat...original	25 g	410	98
water cracker...original	3 g	53	13
KAVLI			
wholegrain crispbread	15 g	198	47
ORGRAN			
corn crispbread	14 g	209	50
REAL FOODS			
corn thins...original	6 g	92	22

	PORTION SIZE	KJ	CAL
RYVITA			
original	20 g	289	69
sesame	20 g	310	74
SUNRICE			
rice cakes...original	6 g	96	23
WOOLWORTHS HOME BRAND			
puffed crispbread	14 g	218	52

sweet biscuits

carob

	PORTION SIZE	KJ	CAL
NATURALLY GOOD (gluten-free)			
soy carob coconut crunch cookies	60 g	1310	313
soy carob ginger gem	60 g	1219	291

chocolate & choc-coated

	PORTION SIZE	KJ	CAL
ARNOTTS			
choc caramel crown	16 g	320	76
choc chip...choc bottom	26 g	531	127
choc mint slice	15 g	340	81
choc monte	35 g	750	179
choc ripple	35 g	690	165
choc tiny teddy	25 g	469	112
tee vee snacks...original	8 g	410	98
tim tam			
double coat	22 g	480	115
original	18 g	400	95

	PORTION SIZE	KJ	CAL
ARTISSE			
organic milk chocolate wafers	20 g	464	111
organic dark chocolate crepes	25 g	474	113
AUSTRALIA'S CHOICE			
decadent choc chip	16 g	341	82
DICK SMITH'S			
temptin' chocolate	18 g	406	97
FREEDOM FOODS			
chocolate blitz	20 g	350	83
chocolate daydream	40 g	784	187
triple treat brownie cookie	28 g	560	134
KRAFT			
oreo	25 g	527	126
LEDA (gluten-free)			
choculence	20 g	428	102
minton	20 g	368	88
McVITIES			
milk/dark chocolate digestives	17 g	353	84
ORGRAN			
gluten-free biscotti...classic choc	7 g	151	36
PARADISE FOOD			
cottage cookies			
chocolate chip indulgence	21 g	426	102
triple choc temptation	21 g	430	103
white choc & macadamia	21 g	439	105
vive cookies			

	PORTION SIZE	KJ	CAL
lites choc chip	10 g	185	44
lites triple choc	10 g	180	43
UNIBIC			
jumbo chocolate chip cookie	60 g	133	32
WEIGHT WATCHERS			
choc chip cookies	14 g	277	66
WOOLWORTHS NAYTURA			
flax snax	34 g	610	146
sugar-free choc orange	20 g	370	88
sugar-free with cocoa bits	20 g	410	98

cookie mix

	PORTION SIZE	KJ	CAL
AUNTIE KATH'S choc chip…made up	18 g	305	73

cream or jam doubles

	PORTION SIZE	KJ	CAL
cream & jam…av. all brands	16 g	330	79
cream-filled…av. all flavours/brands	15 g	295	71
jam-filled…av. all brands	13 g	225	54
wafers (filled)…av. all brands	7 g	155	37
ARNOTTS			
custard cream; delta cream	35 g	740	177
monte carlo	35 g	720	172
premier melting moments	30 g	663	159
triple wafer	35 g	760	182
KEZ'S INDULGENCE			
melting moments	32 g	704	168
PARADISE FOOD			
jam fancies	17 g	313	75

	PORTION SIZE	KJ	CAL
strawberries & cream fancies	21 g	445	106

fruit &/or nut

fruit-filled...av. all brands	15 g	250	60
fruit, iced...av. all brands	12 g	245	59
ARNOTTS			
full o'fruit	31 g	482	115
FREEDOM FOODS			
100 healthy calories apricot temptation	30 g	420	100
blissful berry cookies	28 g	541	129
crunchy coconut	30 g	594	141
sultana splitz	20 g	342	81
KEZ'S INDULGENCE			
almond bread	5 g	87	20
florentines	31 g	583	139
LEDA (gluten-free)			
coconut	20 g	410	98
gingernut	20 g	293	70
golden crunch	20 g	404	97
UNIBIC			
almond biscotti	5 g	97	23

iced

ARNOTTS			
hundreds & thousands	25 g	430	103
iced vo vo	26 g	457	109
tic toc	18 g	330	79
Venetian	35 g	760	181

	PORTION SIZE	KJ	CAL
macaroons & marshmallows			
macaroons...av. all brands	10 g	200	48
marshmallows...av. all brands	17 g	280	67
UNIBIC			
cafe amaretti	7 g	153	37
plain sweet			
polyunsaturated...av. all brands	14 g	250	60
ARNOTTS			
malt o' milk	35 g	670	160
marie	35 g	650	155
milk arrowroot	35 g	640	152
nice	35 g	680	162
Scotch finger	35 g	730	174
ORGRAN			
outback animal vanilla cookies	17 g	298	70
PARADISE FOOD			
anzac	20 g	425	101
butterscotch shortbread	18 g	378	90
cinnamon crunch	20 g	375	89
highland oatmeal	17 g	314	81
malt	16 g	296	71
marie	19 g	340	81
UNIBIC			
anzacs	12 g	259	62
Italian shortbread	19 g	315	75
Parisienne	6 g	132	31

	PORTION SIZE	KJ	CAL
sponge fingers	12 g	147	35
WEIGHT WATCHERS			
butternut	8 g	304	73

savoury biscuits

	PORTION SIZE	KJ	CAL
ALDI			
be light…rice crackers			
mixed; plain	30 g	484	116
spicy	30 g	466	111
ARNOTTS			
cheds	35 g	730	174
clix	15 g	323	77
shapes			
barbecue	25 g	546	130
pizza	25 g	500	119
PARADISE FOOD			
veri deli crackers			
cheddar & chives	25 g	502	110
Italian herb	20 g	388	93
sesame & poppy	25 g	536	128
soy & linseed	21 g	426	102
spring onion	25 g	491	117
SAKATA			
rice crackers…av. all flavours	100 g	1731	413

Cakes, slices, muffins, pancakes

Homemade or not, these guys will seriously hold you back when it comes to losing weight and keeping it off. Because they are high in processed carbs, sugars and fats, they are foods that should only be eaten on special occasions – and in small servings even then. Sometimes the rush of energy we get when eating foods like these that are high in sugar causes our energy levels to crash later, meaning that we look for something else to eat to regain our previous liveliness. Before you know it, you're snacking throughout the day, which is the worst way to keep track of your calorie intake. Always try to keep healthy snacks on hand – fruit and nuts, say – to replace these sugary choices. If you do make your own cakes and muffins, use wholemeal or rice flour and add some flaxseed to the mix, so you are at least getting some nutrients.

	PORTION SIZE	KJ	CAL

cakes

	PORTION SIZE	KJ	CAL
apple strudel	128 g	1120	268
chocolate cake…iced	55 g	825	197
chocolate eclair	70 g	1115	266
cupcake	40 g	620	148
custard tart	135 g	1430	342
date & nut loaf	100 g	1500	359
fruit cake			
boiled	60 g	1015	243
rich	85 g	1145	274
fruit mince slice	150 g	1870	447
jam tart	45 g	670	160
madeira cake	100 g	1480	354
rock cakes	100 g	1670	399
scone…plain	50 g	582	139
sponge cake…iced	60 g	755	180
sweet mince tarts	100 g	1825	436
vanilla slice	135 g	1155	276
MILLS & WARES			
choc roll	50 g	744	178
fruit cake (70% less fat)	100 g	1270	303
jam roll	50 g	653	156
madeira cake	50 g	788	188
MR KIPLING			
bramley apple pies	56 g	809	194

	PORTION SIZE	KJ	CAL
cherry bakewells	40 g	715	171
lemon slices	30 g	514	123
SARA LEE			
Bavarian			
banana caramel	94 g	1301	310
caramel choc	94 g	1341	320
choc swirl	92 g	1345	321
cake			
banana	58 g	855	205
carrot	67 g	1079	258
chocolate	58 g	920	220
cheese cake			
chocolate	100 g	1517	362
mixed berry	103 g	1408	336
strawberry	103 g	1359	324
TOP TASTE			
choc rollettes	28 g	450	107
jam rollettes	28 g	376	90
lamington fingers	20 g	294	70
sponge roll, chocolate	75 g	1172	280
UNIBIC…aniseed cake	23 g	250	60
WEIGHT WATCHERS			
bakery			
cherry bakewells	34 g	523	125
lamington fingers	20 g	278	66

	PORTION SIZE	KJ	CAL

cake & slice mixes

BASCO

	PORTION SIZE	KJ	CAL
multi-purpose mix...for sweet and savoury baking	100 g	1720	410

BETTY CROCKER

devil's food cake	100 g	1510	361

GREEN'S...prepared

entertain

banana coconut	89 g	1440	340
choc on choc	105 g	1600	382
lemon drizzle	93 g	1410	337
orange poppyseed	106 g	1660	398

everyday

carrot	64 g	1030	246
dark chocolate	58 g	864	206
golden butter	65 g	1000	239

MELINDA'S GLUTEN-FREE GOODIES

choc-walnut slice	31 g	656	157
lemon delicious slice	35 g	620	148
passionfruit slice	40 g	789	188

WHITE WINGS...cake mix

banana bread	70 g	900	215
bite-size strawberry babycakes	20 g	340	81
carrot and walnut	105 g	1560	372
choc on choc	73 g	740	177

	PORTION SIZE	KJ	CAL
chocolate cupcakes	63 g	1030	246
orange and poppyseed	75 g	800	191
vanilla cake	75 g	780	186
vanilla cupcakes	64 g	1060	253
WHITE WINGS...slice mix			
double choc fudge brownies	50 g	850	203
smooth caramel slice	44 g	750	179

muffin mixes

	PORTION SIZE	KJ	CAL
BASCO (gluten-free)			
apple & cinnamon	70 g	924	220
double choc	70 g	959	229
BETTY CROCKER			
blueberry...prepared	100 g	1080	258
chocolate chip...prepared	100 g	1083	259
GREEN'S			
blueberry	56 g	627	150
chocolate pantry pack	51 g	515	123
WHITE WINGS (97% fat-free)			
banana honey	60 g	650	155
choc chip	62 g	680	162
triple choc	70 g	1130	270

pancakes & crepes

	PORTION SIZE	KJ	CAL
BASCO...mix			
gluten-free	50 g	496	112

	PORTION SIZE	KJ	CAL
CREATIVE GOURMET...frozen			
French-style crepe	50 g	455	109
GREEN'S...shaker...original	100 g	780	186
ORGRAN...mix			
apple & cinnamon	100 g	1420	339
buckwheat	100 g	1400	335
WHITE WINGS...shaker panjacks			
buttermilk	110 g	810	193
wholemeal	140 g	680	162

scones

	PORTION SIZE	KJ	CAL
homemade			
cheese	45 g	594	142
fruit	50 g	668	160
plain; pumpkin	40 g	582	139
sultana	50 g	775	185
wholemeal	50 g	740	177
packet mix			
ANCHOR LION...classic	50 g	612	146

waffles

	PORTION SIZE	KJ	CAL
NANNA'S	17 g	191	46

Sweet pies & pastries

Despite claims that fruit-based pies are healthy, they're actually high in sugar and fat and shouldn't be on your shopping list if you are serious about managing your weight. The calorie content in these foods is often compounded as most people serve them with cream or ice-cream. Pies are popular choices for holidays or special occasions and they should be limited to these days. Making your own pies can be a way of reducing the calorie count. Using wholemeal flour in the pastry and replacing sugar with low-calorie sweeteners are handy options when baking for the family. Pastries have a tendency to become a habit. Ordering one when you're having a coffee with a friend or grabbing one as a mid-morning snack can easily become a part of your routine. Take the power back and break such habits by consciously choosing healthier, low-calorie alternatives.

	PORTION SIZE	KJ	CAL

pies, sweet

For savoury pies, see **Takeaway Food;
Frozen & Convenience Meals**

	PORTION SIZE	KJ	CAL
fruit	100 g	1553	371
fruit pie with pastry top	100 g	755	180
pumpkin	100 g	885	212
NANNA'S			
crumbles			
apple; blackberry & apple	100 g	936	223
apple & custard	100 g	1100	262
family			
apple	100 g	924	220
apple & custard	114 g	1240	296
apricot	113 g	1110	265
lite apple	119 g	1120	267
lite mixed berry & apple	113 g	1190	284
PAMPAS			
lattice puffs…apple & custard	40 g	524	125
lemon meringue	100 g	106	25
SARA LEE			
apple pie	100 g	1300	310
classic apple…snack	125 g	1621	387
deep dish baked apple pie	133 g	1367	327
light apple…snack	125 g	1351	322

	PORTION SIZE	KJ	CAL

pastry

	PORTION SIZE	KJ	CAL
biscuit crust...raw	100 g	2180	521
choux...baked	100 g	1380	330
filo			
baked	100 g	1560	373
raw	100 g	1180	282
flaky...raw	100 g	1695	405
puff			
baked	100 g	1875	448
raw	100 g	1515	362
shortcrust			
baked	100 g	2045	489
raw	100 g	1735	415
BORG'S			
puff...frozen (non-dairy)	100 g	1370	327
PAMPAS			
filo...chilled	100 g	1380	330
puff	100 g	1370	327
shortcrust...25% reduced fat	100 g	1480	353
sweet tart cases	22 g	410	98
WHITE WINGS...bake			
biscuit bake	100 g	2030	485
pastry mix	100 g	1660	396

	PORTION SIZE	KJ	CAL

pastries, doughnuts, dumplings

croissants

	PORTION SIZE	KJ	CAL
COLES	50 g	1180	282

doughnuts

	PORTION SIZE	KJ	CAL
cinnamon & sugar	50 g	770	184
iced	80 g	1425	341

dumplings

	PORTION SIZE	KJ	CAL
plain	100 g	885	212

pastries

	PORTION SIZE	KJ	CAL
Danish pastry			
apple	67 g	811	193
custard	67 g	845	202
vol-au-vent (case without filling)	100 g	2400	574

Desserts, puddings, dairy snacks

These foods are really high in calories, though you can sometimes find a few low-calorie choices. Jelly is not a bad option for a dessert, but as always, add it to your daily calorie quota. It really doesn't take long for the calories to add up if these foods feature regularly in your diet. One of the times when controlling your calories at dessert can be difficult is when eating out. It's not like you can ask your waiter for a calorie breakdown of your meal! Eating out should be a treat but doesn't have to be a blowout, and dessert, particularly after a starter and a main, can really up your calorie intake for the day. Try sharing a dessert; let's face it, the first few spoonfuls are the best, anyway. But also, if you are full or make a conscious choice not to indulge in dessert, don't feel obliged to order one just because everyone else is; your food choices and calorie control are about you, after all.

	PORTION SIZE	KJ	CAL
desserts			
custard			
baked with cereal	100 g	720	172
banana	100 g	450	108
egg...baked; boiled	100 g	455	109
DAIRY FARMERS			
vanilla...light pouring custard	100 g	316	76
vanilla...thick	100 g	421	101
PAULS			
brandy; vanilla	100 g	432	103
chocolate	100 g	473	113
low fat	100 g	368	88
custard mix			
av. all brands	14 g	200	48
FOSTER CLARK'S...vanilla (made up)	100 g	1470	351
jelly			
made with milk	100 ml	365	87
made with water	100 ml	250	60
AEROPLANE			
jelly lite...av. all flavours	100 g	30	7
COTTEE'S			
standard...av. all flavours	100 ml	280	67
gelatine powder			
av. all brands	10 g	154	36

	PORTION SIZE	KJ	CAL
junket			
av. all brands	100 ml	330	79
puddings			
apple crumble	100 g	1145	274
bread-and-butter pudding	100 g	670	160
Christmas pudding	100 g	1325	317
lemon delicious pudding	100 g	935	223
sponge pudding...jam-filled	100 g	1280	306
steamed pudding...chocolate	100 g	1495	357
trifle	100 g	620	148
COTTEE'S			
instant pudding			
chocolate	130 g	555	132
vanilla	130 g	568	135
SARA LEE			
puddings			
chocolate	79 g	1033	246
sticky date	79 g	1146	273
WHITE WINGS			
rice cream...vanilla (tin)	215 g	900	215
WOOLWORTHS SELECT			
pavlova...classic	100 g	1240	296
pudding mix			
GREEN'S...traditional sponge pudding (made up)			
butterscotch	115 g	788	189

	PORTION SIZE	KJ	CAL
choc	115 g	776	185
lemon	115 g	780	187

dairy snacks

DIVINE CLASSIC

Belgian chocolate	100 g	709	169
creme caramel	100 g	551	131

FOSTER CLARK'S

snak pack

banana; strawberry	140 g	657	157
chocolate; custard cups	140 g	643	154
vanilla	140 g	560	134

FRÛCHE

fromage frais

layers…vanilla on mixed berries	100 g	388	92
tropical mango	100 g	374	88
vanilla creme	100 g	394	94

LION

sago (tin)	215 g	570	136

NESTLÉ

chilled dairy dessert

chocolate mousse	62 g	529	127
diet chocolate mousse	62 g	272	65
diet creme caramel	125 g	317	76
milo	100 g	549	131

	PORTION SIZE	KJ	CAL
YOGO			
dairy dessert			
banana split	100 g	435	103
choc rock	100 g	443	105
swirl…choc & caramel	100 g	440	105
YOPLAIT			
dairy snack			
formé…classic cheesecake	100 g	170	40
le rice…classic vanilla	100 g	464	108

Sweeteners, jams, syrups

When we are looking to make our diets healthier or trying to lose some weight, we can get caught up in just noting the fat content of food. But in some cases it is the sugar component that does the damage. Food manufacturers routinely use what I call 'super sugars' to sweeten their products to make them taste better. The problem is that these sugars – such as sucrose and corn syrup – are refined, manufactured sugars and are generally bad for our health and cause our bodies to store fat. Sugars occur naturally in foods, such as glucose in vegetables and fructose in fruit, and these are easily metabolised by our bodies, giving us energy. The refined sugars are harder to break down and so can cause us to put on weight. Read the labels of food carefully, and always look at the total calorie value. If you see 'sucrose' or 'corn syrup' on the label, alarm bells should start going off.

	PORTION SIZE	KJ	CAL

sugar & sweeteners

fruit concentrates

PUREHARVEST

	PORTION SIZE	KJ	CAL
apple	25 ml	336	80

fruit sugar

fruisana	20 g	340	80

golden syrup

	20 g	251	60

glucose

liquid	100 g	1330	318
powder	100 g	1600	382

malt extract

SAUNDERS'

	35 g	496	118

molasses

black	100 g	900	215
light	100 g	1075	257

palm sugar

Jeeny's oriental foods	100 g	1662	404

sugar

brown sugar; caster sugar; coffee sugar; raw sugar; white sugar	5 g	68	16

sugar cane

juice	100 g	305	73
stem	100 g	250	60

sugar substitutes

equal	1 sachet	3.6	1

	PORTION SIZE	KJ	CAL
equal; hermesetas; sugarella	1 tablet	0.7	0.3
saccharine		0	0
splenda	1 level tsp	8	2
sweetaddin	1 level tsp	68	18
treacle	15 g	182	45

jams & sweet spreads

jam & marmalade

redcurrant jelly…av. all brands	15 g	165	39
BUDERIM			
lemon lime marmalade	15 g	191	45
original marmalade	15 g	192	46
COTTEE'S			
conserve			
blackberry; blackcurrant; strawberry	15 g	169	41
plum	15 g	171	41
marmalade			
breakfast; ginger; mandarin orange	15 g	171	41
IXL			
all about the fruit			
apricot	15 g	131	31
strawberry	15 g	134	32
conserves			
apricot; plum; raspberry; strawberry	15 g	167	40
marmalade	15 g	133	32

	PORTION SIZE	KJ	CAL
ROSES			
marmalade			
lime	15 g	169	40
English breakfast	15 g	172	42
ST DALFOUR			
spreadable fruit			
red raspberry; blackberry; thick apricot;			
black cherry; four fruits	6 g	53	13
WEIGHT WATCHERS			
fruit spread			
apricot; strawberry	15 g	84	20
fruits of the forest	15 g	85	20
YACKANDANDAH			
premium preserves			
raspberry	15 g	172	41
strawberry	15 g	169	40

chocolate spread

	PORTION SIZE	KJ	CAL
FERRERO... nutella	15 g	326	78
SWEET WILLIAM... gluten-; dairy-; nut-free	15 g	330	79

honey

	PORTION SIZE	KJ	CAL
	15 g	255	60

syrups

	PORTION SIZE	KJ	CAL
corn syrup... av. all brands	15 ml	180	43
COTTEE'S... maple-flavoured syrup	15 ml	77	42
GREEN'S... squeeze... maple	15 g	177	42
PUREHARVEST... rice syrup	15 g	41	10

	PORTION SIZE	KJ	CAL

toppings

COTTEE'S

light

caramel	15 g	65	24
chocolate	15 g	21	5

standard

chocolate	15 g	125	30
ice magic	15 g	400	95
strawberry	15 g	100	24
WOOLWORTHS HOME BRAND ... chocolate	15 ml	169	40

icings & frostings

almond paste	20 g	336	80
icing sugar	100 g	1700	407
marzipan	20 g	336	80
CSR ... rich chocolate icing mixture	100 g	1670	399

hundreds and thousands

av. all brands	5 g	65	15

Ice-cream & ice confections

As a special treat I've been known to indulge in some ice-cream on the odd occasion, but I always choose one that is low in calories and low in sugar. Tubs of ice-cream are dangerous as you can just keep going back to the freezer, so if you are having a treat buy a single one. Ice-cream is also something we turn to if we are eating emotionally, so if you know you have a habit of reaching for ice-cream in times of stress, cut off that avenue by not keeping it in the house. Let's face it, even someone with the strongest willpower will eventually succumb if ice-cream is around! There are healthier options as well. One of my favourites is to freeze a banana then blitz it as a healthy, refreshing alternative to ice-cream. You can also make your own lollies; simply put some fresh fruit juice in a plastic cup (not glass or china!), pop a spoon in the top so it makes a handle, and place in the freezer until solid. Perfect for a summer's day.

	PORTION SIZE	KJ	CAL

ice-cream & ice confections

	PORTION SIZE	KJ	CAL
ice-cream cones			
unfilled	5 g	80	19
ESKAL...gluten-free	4 g	61	14
ice-cream			
extra creamy	50 g	538	128
low fat	50 g	160	38
regular	50 g	384	94
BASKIN ROBBINS			
deluxe			
bananas 'n' strawberry	114 g	948	226
chocolate chip	114 g	1123	268
Jamaica almond fudge	114 g	1164	278
mango tango	114 g	1006	240
rum raisin	114 g	1031	246
low-fat			
light...espresso 'n cream	114 g	791	189
low-fat vanilla	114 g	690	165
mango sorbet	114 g	580	138
BULLA			
bars & sticks			
choc bars...vanilla; choc mint; caramel	60 g	724	173
creamy classics			
chocolate	62 g	856	205
vanilla	62 g	854	204

	PORTION SIZE	KJ	CAL
crunches...double choc; rich caramel; honeycomb; vanilla	60 g	755	181
cups...frozen yoghurt...av. all flavours	59 g	310	74
tubs			
frozen yoghurt (97% fat-free)			
mango	100 g	587	140
passionfruit	100 g	592	141
chocolate	100 g	821	196
neapolitan; vanilla	100 g	819	196
CADBURY			
ice-cream bars			
cherry ripe	56 g	716	171
creamy vanilla	64 g	910	217
crunchie	48 g	710	170
flake	73 g	994	974
Fry's Turkish delight	73 g	770	184
picnic	80 g	1179	282
tubs			
honeycomb chocolate with crunchie	100 g	415	99
light chocolate & vanilla	100 g	306	73
light Turkish delight	100 g	338	81
light vanilla	100 g	311	74
triple chocolate	100 g	428	102
CONNOISSEUR			
chocolate obsessions	100 g	833	199
classic vanilla	100 g	943	225

	PORTION SIZE	KJ	CAL
cookie cream commotion	100 g	815	195
DAIRY BELL			
lite…polyunsaturated, no added sugar	100 g	234	56
vanilla…reduced-fat	100 g	320	77
HOMER HUDSON			
chocolate rock	100 g	1170	279
cookies & cream	100 g	1240	296
hoboken crunch	100 g	1250	299
NESTLÉ PETERS			
ice-cream bars/cups			
billabong…chocolate	70 g	395	95
choc wedge			
choc ripple	55 g	710	169
violet crumble	54 g	690	164
dixie cup	51 g	440	105
drumstick			
super choc	78 g	1140	272
vanilla	71 g	940	224
eskimo pie…vanilla	64 g	830	437
frosty fruit			
raspberry split	63 g	285	68
tropical fruit ice	83 g	375	89
heaven…vanilla bean	89 g	1260	300
icypole…raspberry	80 g	200	45
light & creamy			
caramel-flavoured stick	59 g	395	95

	PORTION SIZE	KJ	CAL
vanilla slice	46 g	305	70
milo scoop shake	100 g	820	195
tubs			
extra creamy			
choc honeycomb	100 g	915	220
vanilla	100 g	910	215
light and creamy			
choc vanilla swirl	100 g	680	163
raspberry ripple	100 g	665	160
no sugar added	100 g	455	105
SANITARIUM SO GOOD			
dairy-free bliss			
coconut and mango swirl	100 g	590	141
creamy vanilla	100 g	580	138
heavenly chocolate	100 g	600	143
SARA LEE			
tubs			
absolutely boysenberry	100 ml	840	200
capuccino indulgence	100 ml	739	176
French vanilla	100 ml	843	201
honeycomb & butterscotch	100 ml	915	218
ultra chocolate	100 ml	817	195
STREETS			
bubble o'bill	68 g	1030	246
calippo			
lemon	66 g	359	86

	PORTION SIZE	KJ	CAL
pine lime splice	66 g	565	135
cornetto			
double choc chip	75 g	1272	304
vanilla nut choc	76 g	1286	307
golden gaytime	75 g	1252	299
magnum			
almond	95 g	1444	345
classic	91 g	1294	309
ego caramel	112 g	1489	355
peppermint	91 g	1260	301
paddle pop			
banana	79 g	571	136
chocolate thickshake	126 g	687	164
rainbow	81 g	604	144
tubs			
blue ribbon			
double choc	45 g	836	199
English toffee light	47 g	737	176
frozen fruit yoghurt	70 g	140	33
vanilla	45 g	858	205
vanilla light	45 g	680	162
wildberry light	51 g	700	167
viennetta…vanilla	54 g	1097	262
WEIGHT WATCHERS			
rich chocolate	100 g	635	152

	PORTION SIZE	KJ	CAL
WEISS			
bars			
banana, pineapple & cream	100 g	633	151
hazelnut	100 g	974	233
honey macadamia	100 g	981	234
mango & cream	100 g	603	144
vanilla & raspberries	100 g	758	181
sorbet			
berry	100 g	485	116
lemon	100 g	449	107
mango	100 g	464	111
tubs			
macadamia, mango & cream	100 g	893	213
raspberries & cream	100 g	803	192

Confectionery & snack bars

I have to admit that I do have a bit of a sweet tooth, but as someone who is health and weight conscious I rarely indulge. I usually have something small once a week. Confectionery and snack bars typically contain a lot of sugar and it is this sugar that pumps up the calories. While some sugar in your diet is essential for energy, the refined sugars in confectionary tend to cause our blood sugar levels to rise, which prompts our bodies to store fat. And the way it causes our insulin levels to surge and crash can leave us tired and hungry. So if you are looking to lose weight, knock the sweets on the head. Chocolates and lollies are obviously high in calories and have no nutritional value, so they should only be 'occasional' foods. Children need clear signals that these are not everyday foods, but equally beware of using this type of food as a reward for kids as it potentially can set them up for emotional eating in later life. There are also healthier ways that you can get a kick of sweetness. When I get a craving I turn to berries – nature's confectionery. Raspberries and blueberries should satisfy your need while also giving you essential nutrients and, importantly, fewer calories.

	PORTION SIZE	KJ	CAL

confectionery

generic types

	PORTION SIZE	KJ	CAL
barley sugar	50 g	775	185
caramels			
plain	50 g	830	198
plain with nuts	50 g	895	213
butterscotch	50 g	840	200
chocolate...bar	50 g	1125	269
fudge... chocolate; vanilla	50 g	835	198
halva	50 g	1285	305
liquorice			
allsorts	50 g	732	174
plain	50 g	500	120
marshmallow			
chocolate	50 g	847	201
plain	50 g	675	160
nuts...chocolate-covered	50 g	1116	267
soft sweets (jellies, etc.)	50 g	700	166
turkish delight...no nuts	50 g	314	75

brands

ALLENS

	PORTION SIZE	KJ	CAL
anticol; aniseed	100 g	1620	387
anticol vapour action	100 g	1580	378
butter menthol; echinacea	100 g	1630	389
butter menthol...plus honey	100 g	1590	380

	PORTION SIZE	KJ	CAL
kool...mint	100 g	1670	399
minties	100 g	1580	377
soothers...all flavours	100 g	1620	387
XXX mints	100 g	1590	380
ARTISSE			
organic			
dark chocolate with almonds	50 g	1120	268
extra dark chocolate	50 g	1160	277
milk chocolate	50 g	1170	279
no added sugar			
dark chocolate	50 g	960	229
milk chocolate	50 g	1025	245
CADBURY			
assortments			
favourites	100 g	2020	483
milk tray	100 g	2080	497
roses	100 g	1930	461
bars			
cherry ripe	55 g	1062	253
crunchie	50 g	1015	242
flake	30 g	672	160
time out	40 g	892	213
twirl	42 g	941	224
chocolate blocks			
dairy milk	100 g	2210	528
dream	100 g	2350	561

	PORTION SIZE	KJ	CAL
fruit and nut	100 g	2100	501
hazelnut	100 g	2280	544
old gold	100 g	2150	514
peppermint	100 g	2000	478
snack	100 g	2010	480
top deck	100 g	2270	542
children's			
caramello koala	20 g	410	98
freddo	12 g	265	63
CHUPA CHUPS...all flavours	12 g	200	50
CÔTE D'OR			
bouchee	25 g	555	133
FRY'S turkish delight	55 g	886	211
GREEN & BLACKS			
organic/fairtrade chocolate			
dark	100 g	2289	551
maya gold	100 g	2194	526
milk	100 g	2184	523
LIFESAVERS			
musk; spearmint	100 g	1680	402
pepomint	100 g	1670	399
LINDT			
excellence			
dark 70 %	100 g	2180	520
dark chilli; dark mint intense	100 g	2120	510
dark orange intense	100 g	2080	500

	PORTION SIZE	KJ	CAL
MASTERFOODS			
bagged confectionery			
fantales	100 g	1840	440
jaffas	100 g	1960	469
smarties	100 g	2000	476
bounty	50 g	1020	244
dove			
caramel	100 g	2100	502
dark	100 g	2270	542
hazelnut	100 g	2230	532
milk	100 g	2290	547
m&m			
milk	25 g	513	123
peanut	25 g	543	130
maltesers	45 g	943	225
mars...bar			
regular	60 g	1150	275
lite	45 g	740	177
milky way...choc whip	100 g	1860	444
skittles	55 g	935	223
snickers	60 g	1230	294
starburst			
babies...30% less sugar	25 g	283	68
fruit chews	58 g	828	198
gummi jumble	50 g	652	156
rattlesnakes...30% less sugar	25 g	283	68

	PORTION SIZE	KJ	CAL
twix	100 g	2110	504
MENTOS			
fruit; mint; spearmint	3 g	44	10
NATURAL CONFECTIONERY CO., THE			
dinosaurs; forbidden fruit; jelly babies;			
mixed jellies; snakes	100 g	1420	339
licorice sticks	100 g	1510	361
soft chews	100 g	1630	390
soft jellies...fruit salad	100 g	1390	332
sours...squirms	100 g	1390	332
NESTLÉ			
bars			
aero	6 g	152	36
golden rough	20 g	450	107
kit kat			
4 finger mint	45 g	500	119
4 finger original	45 g	980	234
chunky	60 g	1320	315
chunky caramel	60 g	1370	327
chunky cookies & cream	60 g	730	174
milo bar	50 g	1160	277
mint pattie	20 g	360	86
chocolate blocks			
club original	20 g	430	103
double blend	20 g	460	109
fruit & almond	20 g	450	107

	PORTION SIZE	KJ	CAL
snacks			
starz…dunkaroos…choc hazelnut	22 g	480	115
OVALTEENIES	15 g	223	53
PASCAL			
bagged confectionery			
caramels	100 g	2100	501
clinkers	100 g	1985	474
columbines	100 g	1807	432
eclairs	100 g	1855	443
licorice allsorts	100 g	1560	372
RED TULIP			
after dinner mints	25 g	450	107
TIC TAC			
orange	100 g	1632	384
peppermint	100 g	1671	393
spearmint; extra strong	100 g	1658	390
TOBLERONE			
milk chocolate	100 g	2200	526
WALCO			
quick-eze	100 g	870	208
WRIGLEY			
chewing gum			
standard…with sugar			
hubba bubba	7 g	85	20
juicy fruit	1.4 g	18	4
pk	1.4 g	18	4

	PORTION SIZE	KJ	CAL
sugarfree… extra			
liquid blast	2 g	20	5
peppermint	2 g	16	4
strawberry	2 g	19	4
eclipse mints…sugarfree			
orange; spearmint	2 g	28	7
peppermint	2 g	29	7

snack bars

fruit & nut bars

ARTISSE

	PORTION SIZE	KJ	CAL
organic snack bars			
café latte	40 g	752	180
cranberry crunch	40 g	711	170
nougat	40 g	669	160
proactive flax	40 g	711	170
seed delight	40 g	711	170

EUROPE

	PORTION SIZE	KJ	CAL
honey nougat log	45 g	882	210
summer roll	45 g	905	216

LEDA NUTRITION

	PORTION SIZE	KJ	CAL
gluten/dairy-free bars			
apricot	42 g	573	137
banana	42 g	600	143

UNCLE TOBY'S

fruit breaks bars

	PORTION SIZE	KJ	CAL
apple raspberry	33 g	530	127
mixed berry; apricot; apple	33 g	520	124
rollups			
funprints…strawberry	16 g	230	55
rainbow…berry berry	16 g	240	57
fruit salad	15 g	230	55

muesli & cereal bars

KELLOGG'S

	PORTION SIZE	KJ	CAL
crunchy nut cereal bars			
mixed nut	30 g	669	160
peanut	30 g	663	158
k-time twists			
raspberry & apple	37 g	510	122
strawberry & blueberry; apple & cinnamon	37 g	500	119
k-time muffin bars…apple	37 g	510	122
LCMs…rice bubble treats with choc chip	22 g	390	93
nutri-grain bar	30 g	520	124

UNCLE TOBY'S

	PORTION SIZE	KJ	CAL
chewy	31 g	540	129
crunchy			
apricot	20 g	360	86
original	20 g	390	93
yoghurt topps			
apricot; raspberry; mango; honeycomb	31 g	570	136
strawberry	31 g	560	134

Acknowledgements

The publisher would like to thank the manufacturers who have contributed nutritional and content information about their products.

Data for the nutrient composition of Australian meats, fruits and vegetables are copyright to Associate Professor Heather Greenfield, R.B.H. Wills and other authors at the Department of Food Science and Technology, University of New South Wales, and are reproduced and used with permission.

Thanks to Yvonne Colley, for her patient research and product updates, Suzanne Gibbs and Louise Keats for nutrition and cooking information, and also Joanna McMillan Price and Clare Collins.

crunch time

crunch time cookbook

losing the last 5 kilos

5 minutes a day

no excuses cookbook

everyday weight loss

your best body

superfoods cookbook

www.penguin.com.au/michellebridges